Boy George on Boy George

"It's very difficult to explain why you suddenly decide not to look like everyone else. But from a very early age, I thought everyone looked awful."

"When I first dyed my hair, my father just looked over his paper and said, 'That what you want? It's what you have.'"

"My ambition was to be in every single newspaper in the country...being famous for doing nothing was good fun."

"I am not a great singer: I'm a vocalist and a copyist. If I hear something I can copy and adapt. I know how to caress words."

"The basic reason I'm successful is that Culture Club makes good music."

—all quotes by Boy George, from the interview in *Rolling Stone* by Nancy Collins

Boy George

by Scott Cohen

BERKLEY BOOKS, NEW YORK

BOY GEORGE

A Berkley Book / published by arrangement with the author

PRINTING HISTORY
Berkley edition / May 1984

ISBN: 0-425-07639-3

Material from this book has been gathered in first-hand personal interviews, and information from the following sources: *Event* magazine, *Creem*, *Rolling Stone*, *Trouser Press*, *Star Hits*, *Smash Hits*, *New Sounds*, *News of the World*, The (London) *Sun*, The (London) *Daily Mirror*, The (London) *Daily Star*, *Weekly World News*, *U.S.* magazine, *People* magazine, *Aquarian* magazine, *Newsweek* magazine, *Los Angeles Times*, New York *Daily News*, *No. 1*, *The Face*, *New Music Express*, *Melody Maker*, *Village Voice*, *Musician* magazine, *Billboard*, MTV, *Rockbill*, *Rock Report*, *Detroit Free Press*, *Boston Rock*, *Washington Post*, *The New Paper*, *Cleveland Plain Dealer*, *Rolling Stone* Radio Guest D.J.-Dan Formento, *Freeze Frame*, *Unicorn Times*, *Philadelphia Daily News*, *The New Yorker*, *Connecticut* magazine, *USA Today*.

Contents

Introduction 11
1 A Boy is Born 15
2 End to "Normalcy" 21
3 From Punk to Ted and Beyond 27
4 Green Face, Red Neck, Purple Hair 35
5 "Face-About-Town" 43
6 Lieutenant Lush 49
7 Almost a Star 57
8 Culture Club 65
9 White Boy 69
10 Boy George 77
11 Do You Really Want to Hurt Me? 87
12 Top of the Pops 95
13 Colour by Numbers 107
14 CCC 113
15 America 123
16 Boy George Today 143
17 Boy George on Boy George 147

Boy George

Introduction | |

An artist is at work and the canvas is his own face.

The hand applying the touches is sure and deft, like that of a master etcher.

First, the eyebrows are shaved off. Suddenly the features stand out, as they do on a Kabuki mask. In place of the discarded eyebrows, delicate arches are drawn on in heavy black eyebrow pencil.

The face is covered with bright white foundation. The effect is ghostly until, with the brown makeup stick shading the jawline, definition returns, so that the face no longer looks ghostly but rather rigid, abstract.

The skull and eyes are emphasized by shading the line of the cheekbones.

The line going up into the temples and hairline is touched up with black shading powder.

The same hand outlines the eyes—a solid black loop from the corner of the eye around the inside and around the outer lashes. Top and bottom, black mascara is applied. A gold-shine eye shadow highlights the eyes, brows and lids, which glisten then like gold leaf plated on fixtures.

Next, the mouth, which forms a perfect *V* on the top lip. A black pencil tracing over it exaggerates the shape; then it's filled in with flaming lipstick, changing the mouth so that it is but a large, polished, brilliant jewel, an object rather than something of flesh.

The face, foundation, shadowing and makeup are protected by a translucent face powder the way fixative, sprayed over a pastel drawing, protects it from smudging.

The hair is left to the end. It has the same unreal look as the mouth. It is darkish brown with bright streaks of blue and red, falling well beneath the shoulders in a tangle. The hands of the artist stroke the hair, catching one strand, then another, plaiting them and garnishing them, one after another, with multi-colored ribbons, beads and bangles.

The work of art is completed.

Slipping into a billowy, colorful dress, Boy George is ready to go out on stage.

While Boy George has been plucking and lining, shadowing and painting on the surface that is his own face, fans of all ages have been lining up outside the Joe Louis Arena in Detroit. Here in the heart of Motown they've come to see this outrageous singer and his band called Culture Club.

On this, Boy George's third American tour, it is clear from the size of the crowd that the answer to the question of whether Americans have taken to him is no longer in doubt.

"I admire Boy George," one teenage boy waiting in line

says, "because he's not intimidated by anybody." Another says, "He's the wave of the future."

The girls say, "He's great. He's fantastic."

Do they think he is sexy?

"Absolutely!"

The comments above are typical of those made by Boy George fans all over the world. His most obvious feature, his androgyny, is accepted by everyone. In America he's heard on Top 40, rock, disco, new music, adult and black radio stations. There is talk of his making movies. In England he is the "Personality of the Year." Japan loves him. In the few parts of the world where he's not considered an international superstar, he's pronounced a symptom of degeneracy and decline.

In the three years that Culture Club has been together they've astounded the music business. Their album "Kissing To Be Clever" was the first debut album in the two decades since the Beatles to produce three singles in the Top Ten, and their follow-up album, "Colour By Numbers," was just as popular. Culture Club has sold over five million albums in the U.S.; with singles sales, the total number of records sold comes to ten million. After five Top Ten hits in a row, the band took the 1984 Grammy, and, via satellite from London, Boy George accepted the music industry's Best New Artist award, obviously enjoying his love affair with the world.

1
A Boy
is Born

Boy George was born in a bland, spiritless blue collar suburb of which there are dozens in and around London. On June 14, 1961, Jeremiah and Diana O'Dowd welcomed into their growing family the baby boy they named George Alan.

The proud parents were, of course, unaware that the baby cries they heard would grow into the aching, breathy voice that, two decades later, would capture the hearts of people all over the world. Jeremiah was an ex-army officer, now in the building trade, whose hobby was coaching boxers. Perhaps at that moment, seeing the baby in his mother's arms, he had hopes of making him a pugilist. Two of his sons did materialize this wish, growing up to become fighters. As a very young child, George himself took boxing lessons at his dad's club. For three years he did the exercising and the training. But he wouldn't fight, and he gave up boxing altogether the moment he became aware that his father's ideas would never suit him.

The O'Dowds were Irish Catholics living in Bexleyheath in South London. The development of this district dates back to the nineteenth century, when Bexley began to flourish as a residential area close to the metropolis. Many parks and woodlands dotted the district and remained intact, while in subsequent years the area changed and became largely working-class. These woods proved a boon to George as a child when playing hookey from school or when he just wanted to escape his home.

George Alan was the third son and he was followed by two more brothers and a sister. His early years were spent in a crowded three-room house that stood at Joan Crescent in Eltham. Along with the six kids there were two pet Alsatians. Mum and Dad occupied one room. George shared his with his brothers Richard, Kevin, Gerald, and David. His sister, Siobhain, had a tiny room of her own.

Living in a large family at close quarters had an enduring effect on him. He would always need to be with people— for warmth, support, security. The songs he writes today are collaborative; he needs the tension, the excitement, the talk—the endless talk—involving the whole band. He needs to argue, to hear chatter and to hear himself chatter. He worked best amidst noise and distraction because he's always lived that way, first with his family and then on the streets. He cannot be solitary. He can only be creative when he talks, argues, interacts.

As a child, George was very temperamental, loving one minute, hateful the next. His temper tantrums turned the house upside down. A lot was likely to get to him. Extremely sensitive, easily hurt, he was constantly angry because he felt that he was always being misunderstood. In a tantrum he'd slam doors, throw things around and scream.

At this time, however, he was not yet considered a "problem child." That assessment from the parents would come a few years later, when their son began prancing around the house in lurex cat suits, platform shoes, Indian scarves and spiky purple hair. But before that happened, the problem child was his brother Richard, the eldest, a "skinhead," who was always getting into trouble. After being a skinhead, Richard adopted the "droog" look like the psychopaths in "Clockwork Orange," and then Richard simply vanished for seven years.

The difficulties at home were complicated by the lean times in the building trade. Eventually, Jeremiah's business would pick up, but, for a while, bringing in money for a wife and six children was an almost hopeless struggle. After a hard day's work, he came home weary and irritable, in a mood in which small things upset him, and there was constant rowing in the house.

At home the emotions of eight people boiled as if in a stew over which hung the spectre of poverty. "I hate you," George would yell at his father—the word "hate" was often on his lips. There was terrible shouting, his father slamming the table and bellowing, "You have no right to talk like that to me!" And George roaring, "Oh yes I do!" He hated his father's anger, not comprehending the lean times in the building trade and the frustration of being responsible for feeding the brood; he saw only the coarseness and sterility.

Occasionally at dinner with his skinhead son and the other children ranged noisily round the table, Jeremiah was unable to contain himself. He'd flare up, George would throw his plate full of food on the floor and all hell would break loose. Diana O'Dowd usually had *her* set-to at breakfast, where George had the habit of dawdling out the minutes until he would be late for school. Once she dragged him from his chair and forced him out of the house. As he retreated down the street, George shot back at the top of his voice, "I hate you!" As usual, a few minutes later he was terribly sorry.

The stormy atmosphere at the O'Dowds came to a head when George was fourteen. One day he had an argument with his father that surpassed all the others. It ended with George locking himself in the bathroom. His father forced the door open. Escaping with a cut foot, George made for the house of a friend's, where he stayed two weeks. Finally his mother called and asked him to come home. George loved her very much. His dad also got on the phone, sounding chastened and contrite, promising that everything would be all right. And true enough, from that day the home, though still far from peaceful, became different. George made up with his mum and dad and everything was fine.

The trouble was that he had to vie for his parents' affection with five siblings. All children need love; some, however, need more than others, and George was one of those. He wanted all his parents' love and felt deeply hurt in an uncomprehending way when they failed to pay attention to this deep and crying need. Affection—constant affection—was all he wanted, and because he felt the lack of love, he sensed the world's sin, which was indifference. So he grew up as an insecure child, and from insecurity he grew selfish, manipulative, stormy, difficult. All his life he would try to fill that void he had felt as a child by having the world stand up and pay attention to little George O'Dowd, the Irish builder's son.

George has now come to realize that his relationship with his parents had been far more complex than he had thought. His father was "a very loving person." The love had been there but had been unexpressed. Now he is able to see how in struggling with life his father's finer qualities had become stunted. As a child, Boy George had only known that he never wanted to be like Jeremiah. But now he can respect him, even love him. He says, "I can kiss him now. I couldn't when I was a kid—and that sort of thing you really want to do when you can't."

2
End to
"Normalcy"

When George entered his teens he began to wear strange outfits and even stranger hairdos. The first time he dyed his hair orange his father just stared over his paper in shock. George tottered around the house in immensely high platform shoes. He wore huge flared trousers with velvet cutouts and a cravat draped like bunting around his neck. These outfits were not quite so exotic as the stilt-like stiletto heels and the straw hats covered with fruit and birds that he would come to favor later on. But they were enough to cause tension in the house and with the neighbors.

As his parents saw it, what made it worse was that George was being supported by Aunt Josie, the eccentric one in the family. She entirely approved of George's tastes. She encouraged him to "wear his fantasies." To a psychologist, George's crazy outfits would have seemed his way of escaping a stifling, colorless environment. But Boy George says that he never felt he was escaping anything, that it was all perfectly normal. His home life had nothing to do with it; as far as that went, his upbringing had been "very normal." Dressing up was something he liked to do, and if he liked to do something it was no longer an issue. It had nothing to do with being "disturbed," as some might see it. He was the same as everyone else, except that he liked to dress up and thought boys and girls were more similar than different.

With the same platform shoes, flared trousers, cravat and a big floppy hat, he went to church every Sunday. He did not see the connection between worshipping and what kind of clothes a person wears. Everybody, including the Church, would have to take him as he was. It took a long time for his parents to understand that. Often his mother was in the front room pulling shirts off his back, begging him not to wear them. She absolutely forbade him wearing his hair in a corkscrew, and when threats and ridicule and everything else failed, she went to work with reverse psychology. In Petticoat Lane, she bought the highest platform shoes she could find, telling George they were for school and hoping that after being sent home he would disavow them. What she had foreseen happened, though without the hoped-for result. The headmaster duly sent him home, but George refused to give up his platforms.

Music and clothes first made their impact on British youth in the Carnaby Street explosion—garish fashions, long hair, hippies, mods and rockers, rhythm and blues and the Beatles, the Rolling Stones, the Kinks, the Yardbirds and many now forgotten bands playing in scores of clubs that had sprouted overnight from Soho to Eel Pie Island on the

Thames. A decade later, when George O'Dowd was thirteen years old and preening himself in South London, the process was repeating itself under the banner of "glam rock" when all the "groovers" tried to model themselves on Ziggy Stardust and the glittery, orange-haired, sexually ambiguous image of David Bowie.

George acquired his first pop fashion idol from the "glam rock" scene, Marc Bolan of Tyrannosaurus Rex, who wore velvet and glitter. Bolan, coming from the Streets, was his kind of hero, and under Bolan's influence George's closets began to bulge with embroidered jackets, gauzy skirts, tunic trousers and Indian scarves.

Bolan was his fashion role model, but musically he fell under the spell of David Bowie. He saw his first Bowie concert in 1973. Several of his emotions were aroused, the strongest being admiration and envy.

By the time George got to see him, Bowie had already toned down his androgynous act, but enough remained to leave a lasting impression on George. The androgyny that became his own mark as a singer dates back to this obsession with Bowie.

Meanwhile, a big change was taking place in the family. The O'Dowd's were moving from their cramped house at Joan Crescent. For years Mum had been prodding the housing council for a bigger house, being all that time ignored, until one day she simply stopped paying rent. The council relented and jubilantly the whole family transported itself a few miles north to Shooters Hill. There they still only had three bedrooms, but the rooms were much larger and seemed even more spacious when Richard, after a disagreement with his mother, left home.

At Shooters Hill George fell for his first girl. It was not

a matter of the heart, however; it was more a matter of being impressed by how she looked and carried herself. Her name was Tracie Birch. She wore a sea-green Vidal Sassoon haircut and garish make-up. Her clothes consisted of glaring odds and ends cut in the strangest shapes. Her body was not fully developed; she had a wistful look; and like a jackdaw she picked up all sorts of shiny objects and planted them on herself.

The influence of Tracie on George was instantaneous and overwhelming. George was capable of reacting only in one way—with enthusiasm—or not at all. His desires were either obsessive or did not exist at all. Thus his feelings for Tracie affected him profoundly.

When he returned to school after the summer holidays the teachers did not recognize him. Gone was the long hair—it had been cut into a wedge and dyed a bright, day-glo orange. Also gone were the platforms, replaced by plastic sandals. He wore his trousers skintight. There was no collar to his shirt and around his neck was a thin tie like the one Bowie wore, except that George had cut his in half.

From that day, his school career went crashing downhill. He had liked English and art but his progress was impeded because of the time he spent arguing with his teachers. He hated school because at school they taught "normalcy." You were educated not to have a personality and they were very cruel to anyone who was different. If the headmaster could wear a gown and a board and a tassel, George did not see why he should be penalized for wearing platforms or a half-tie.

For being "different" George was repeatedly punished. At last he was sent up to the Greenhouse, the special room for incorrigibles at the top of the school, where those considered problem students had to sit out their time until they reached school-leaving age. In the Greenhouse there was a psychologist at whom the incorrigibles cursed and swore openly. The head of the "Special Needs Department" was another target; Boy George particularly hated him.

The inevitable happened one day. In September of 1976 he came home with a note from the headmaster saying that George had been "argumentative and insolent toward the head of the Special Needs Department," and that the school found it "impossible to contain him." His parents were advised that they had the right to appeal by writing to the officer of the district. But the parents never appealed. Jeremiah took the envelope in which the note was contained and phlegmatically marked it, "Stage 1. George is expelled. Career continues."

As the headmaster's action had long been expected, his parents took the news calmly. Further talk would be futile, and ten days later, his school career over, George was happy because there was nothing he wanted to be except "different"—different from what parents, society and school thought he should be. He loved his "difference"; he saw it and rejoiced each time he looked in the mirror where the image cast back showed not George O'Dowd, a runty fifteen-year-old with a rather big nose and weak chin, but a thousand beings of romance, nightmare, dream and fantasy, and at the end great riches, renown and a world at his feet.

3

From Punk to
Ted and Beyond

In 1982, on his first U.S. tour, Boy George was constantly running into women who would gasp in surprise, "My God, you're so big!" America's newest sensation learned to shrug it off, bemused by the fact that everywhere he went people expected a midget to get out of the car. In fact, Boy George is far from an undersized lightweight. Standing over six feet tall, with an athletic build, he has thick arms, powerful legs, big bones, and despite the pink or blue eyeliner, the flaming red lipstick and pancake makeup, he can, by his own accounts, throw a mean punch. At fifteen, when the school doors closed behind him for good, he was virtually full-grown. And as an additional mark of being grown-up he had kissed his first girl.

Her name was Brenda and the experience lives on in one of his early songs and the title of Culture Club's debut album, "Kissing To Be Clever." Though the song by the same title was soon dropped from the repertoire—"it was *really* naive," says Boy George today—the memory, and, more important, the feeling, became etched on his mind.

The event took place at one of his brother's parties, where Brenda pulled him aside and made her play. He had never kissed a girl before, and in kissing her he experienced pleasure. At that age all pleasure is highly charged, but George sensed that something was lacking. He did not feel rapture, and he wanted to feel rapture; being "romantic," an extremist in all things, he wanted to be shaken to the depths, instead of "kissing to be clever."

Not Brenda, but a pixie-faced girl with a short, pre-punk haircut, was his true love in those days. Her name was Shelley Hughes. She was his longest-lasting girlfriend, who admired his clothes, his colorful hair and his humor. Shelley did not at all mind that with his orange hair and crazy clothes she could not show her boyfriend in the local pub. Even back then, George's sexuality, like his clothes, did not figure as something to unduly concern him.

His contradictory stance on his sexuality was not often understood. He thought it amusing—"a giggle"—and he liked the attention he was getting. That was more important than sex. Sex was nothing like the triumph of being sought after and feeling wanted. It felt extraordinary to be desired. But he was still a Roman Catholic, and he knew that he shouldn't be doing the sort of things he was doing. Yet he continued because this was before punk, when nothing much else was happening in London. So what he did was a "giggle," it was "funny," and it was something that met the needs of an uncertain fourteen-year-old boy without money who restlessly roamed the streets at night. And when sometimes he hung out all night at a club, he would tell his mother that he had spent the night at a friend's.

He would make his astonishing appearance with orange hair in London clubs like Louise's, where he became a regular, and Visuals, one of his favorite haunts. There were also the Global Village, Shaguaramas, the Goldmine and, on his old turf of Bexleyheath, the Black Prince. A whole generation of fourteen- and fifteen-year-olds like him discovered the adult world through this immersion into the night world of London's drearier suburbs. Most were school dropouts, unskilled, uneducated, often jobless, always bored. They wandered into those blaring, steamy, poorly lit clubs in search of excitement. All their efforts to look original were pathetic and sad. But George was not like them. He stood out because he was not pathetic but striking, not at all sad but sharp-tongued and funny. To be noticed he had to be extreme; he had to be extreme to be valued for his individuality and to express this individuality he looked strikingly "weird."

That was the difference between himself and David Bowie, George discovered. He was always comparing himself to his idol, and his insight meant his first emancipation from the thrall of Ziggy Stardust—that Bowie met people who "made him weird," while he, George O'Dowd, had been weird "from the beginning."

George O'Dowd was not the only example of "weirdness" to be found in certain London clubs at the time. In this twilight period before "punk," the first outrages were being seen on the streets. There were lots of fourteen- and fifteen-year-olds who looked just as "weird" as he did, though in a different way, youngsters who did not know that they were forerunners of the coming fashion. When one day he went to the station to welcome back David Bowie from his tour of America, George was astounded to see this freaky-looking crowd. He had not realized how many weird people there were, and it stimulated him.

George came onto this scene just when punk was becoming the rage. It was a vague social protest by adolescents against futility and boredom. It began in the lower and working classes, where life was ugly, and this ugliness, adopted by youngsters who would never have expensive clothes, was made defiant and menacing.

But he never became a "punk" in the accepted sense. He did not put safety pins in his nose or ears, nor would he put on a cut-off T-shirt to display a pale, thin, hairless, adolescent stomach. Two things militated against his becoming a full-fledged punk. One was the punk cult of violence. The other was the punk cult of ugliness.

From thousands of hours of studying himself in the mirror, Boy George has always been aware of his physical imperfections—as the lead vocalist of Culture Club he wears loose billowy outfits to conceal thick arms and legs. But back in the mid-seventies, when he was a skinny sixteen-year-old, he only felt that the punk look was too colorless to be becoming. Also, punks liked to underscore their physical blemishes, making their unappealing features even less appealing, and George wanted to look attractive—strange and "weird," but attractive. When he began using makeup it was because he thought it would make his face prettier. He dyed his hair because he believed that a purple or orange color suited him better than the natural mousey color. Punks would look for clothes in a junk store and pick out the most hideous rags. Boy George was not like that. He liked his clothes bizarre because they were part of a fantasy that made him strange and beautiful, and once launched as a celebrity he would design and assemble his own tentlike dresses and put on a Hasidic bowler and satin ballet slippers and apply tons of makeup and put his hair in dreadlocks because that was his fantasy, and all his fantasies, being his own, were beautiful.

One thing about the punk phenomenon, however, struck him forcefully. Punk was not fashion, but *anti*-fashion fashion. That's what he liked about it. Regular fashion was boring. Seeing himself in normal clothes in childhood photographs he thought he looked ridiculous. Punk clothes were not ridiculous but still boring. As a concession to the punk look, he wrapped dog chains around his body—at fifteen, having not yet formulated his own style, he was still hesitant. All he knew was that he did not want to be a follower. He would wear what he liked and then he wanted people to follow him. He could only be satisfied by setting the trend himself.

George got to know punk fashion in depth by spending nearly a year in the London clothing mecca that runs along Chelsea's King's Road. Through a friend he got a job as a sales boy at a place called Shades.

Though a couple of shops on the King's Road had just begun selling punk wear, Shades did not go all-out for it, keeping on hand such "conservative" items as Glenn Miller suits and winkle-pickers. George liked the job. The Chelsea Antique Market, where Shades was located, provided an excellent observation post to watch the flow of what was in and what was out and what was the last word in clothing. And though as yet he had no inkling of his own musical career, the racks of Shades brought George into contact with the world of pop music. One day he was thrilled to meet Bob Marley, the King of Reggae, having little idea that the Jamaican sound would become an important ingredient in Culture Club's catchy eclectic sound.

But music, and even less so his own involvement in it, was hardly in the forefront of his mind just then. His chief obsession remained clothes, because clothes attracted attention, and attention was what he was avidly seeking. Each time he saw someone looking like no one else, he'd study the look and try to go it one better. Thus, meeting Philip Salon at a club called Bangs became a turning point. Salon was a club regular, sporting black lips and horns. He wore a skirt, pit boots and leather gloves. Around his neck he had a paper toilet seat liner. George was terribly impressed; Salon was "brilliant."

This breathtaking apparition was to become his best friend. Philip Salon gave him the courage to wear dresses. He acquired from Philip, who thought nothing of wearing suspenders and shorts with a top hat, the confidence to try on anything whatsoever, to experiment, to create and to critically calculate the startling effect he had on others.

Meeting the "brilliant" Salon was important to George in that it came at a time when he was becoming disenchanted with the punk look. Not the least of this disenchantment was caused by the habit punks had of punching each other in the mouth. They used this greeting instead of shaking hands. In this respect, at least, George found that he was traditional. He was violent only in his emotions and obsessions; otherwise, he was peaceable, wishing only to be admired and paid attention.

From the punks George turned to another group that was then competing for dominance on the streets. These were the Teddy Boys or Teds. At his age, he still felt the need to belong. He was not yet ready to fly on his own wings, the raggedy, flapping, oversized "wings" made of bedspreads or sacking cloth which five years later would turn him into the notorious Boy George. And having become anti-punk, but still wanting to "belong," his only alternative was the Teds, the sworn enemies of punks.

In actuality, there was not much to choose between them, except in point of dress. The Teds looked like Marlon Brando in the Wild One, with black leather jackets and "bovver" boots. They liked to hoist with old-fashioned suspenders the tops of their jeans as closely as possible to their jawlines. Their hair came in two basic styles—close-cropped a la skinhead, or in a "quiff," that is, a spitcurl in front and "DA" in back.

George put on a leather jacket. He styled his hair in a "quiff," and to complete the effect, he whipped out a drawing pencil, though not to put arches over his plucked eyebrows as routinely as he would later on. As a Ted he used the pencil to trace a racy mustache on his upper lip.

He loved this Ted image of himself. He was pleased with the "quiff," and mustache. But soon the "quiff" went and he wiped the pencil mustache from his lip. What turned him against the Teds and caused his break with them was their "attitude." The Teds, like the punks, were violent. They liked to go out on the streets and do things like "Paki-bashing," beating up Pakistanis, or kicking people with their "bovver" boots for fun.

Feeling "different" himself, George understood others who were "different," and when Culture Club was formed, the name was meant to show that culture was the harmony of differences.

4

Green Face, Red Neck, Purple Hair

"I had nothing when I was younger—no money, no future. I was always interested in celebrities, and I was desperate to become one."

When Boy George spoke these words, reminiscing about his deprived childhood, he had broken through to fame in the U.S. with his hit album "Kissing To Be Clever." Culture Club had been enthusiastically received on the native ground of rock, as the sales figures convincingly showed. The band's pop-sounding riffs with the now-and-again zippy reggae twists appealed to an across-the-board American audience. The satiny, sweet and misty voice of the rock crooner was being hailed as the great new sound of the year. Nevertheless, for all the praise showered on the songs and the "back-to-basics" danceable tunes, the American press was more interested in Boy George's makeup kit than his music.

"Boy George has shown the world what talent, a little eyeliner and lipstick can do" was a typical headline.

The ironic part about the U.S. media fascination was that by the time Boy George "hit" in America, his appearance was already quite sober, considering what it had been. For several years before his U.S. debut, Boy George, without singing a note and without one musical lick, had been a top celebrity in England, vying for prominence in the English media only with Princess Di.

"Before I started Culture Club," Boy George explained on his American tour, "I didn't have any money whatsoever, so I thought, 'Well, I'll have to become very well known so that I can chat my way into everything for free.' So I went out of my way to be the most outrageous person in the world. I'm quite tame now compared to what I used to be like." What he used to be like, he said, was "really loony."

His instant stardom could not have happened in America, Boy George believes, because in England you can be a celebrity and have nothing to sell. "You have a lot of minor celebrities there," he says, "who don't really do anything; they just have weird haircuts and nice clothes, and people put them in magazines. In America, it's based more on how much money you have and what kind of car you drive. In England, young people up from the gutter can become famous. I used to get in everywhere for free."

After leaving school, George O'Dowd made up his mind that he really didn't want to have a job, but that if he went out to find one he'd go "dressed up"—and if he didn't get hired, it would be no great loss. This attitude led to a lot of friction at home. By then, his parents had become resigned to their son's "differentness," but they were still dead set against his attitude. They tried to reason and came up with a compromise, "Do something to get a job and *then* dress up." But their counsel fell on deaf ears. Life without "dressing up" would not be worth living for George.

George's drive for celebrity status began in earnest when after nine months with Shades he quit his job because of the low pay. It had been the longest-lasting job he would ever hold.

He realized that he would never be able to count on regular employment after next working one week in a fruit-packing plant. He was given the sack because the management considered his appearance "disturbing." George had liked one thing about that job—it had provided him with plenty of the paper bags the plant used for packing, which he tried to fashion into items of apparel. He couldn't help wanting to put on his person whatever lay close at hand.

After losing this job he entered fully into the life of the streets. And there he would remain for the next five years until Culture Club had its first success.

There were numbers of kids like him, "dropouts" who couldn't or didn't want to fit in, and they lived in abandoned buildings, and on unemployment. George moved into the first of numerous abandoned buildings. He also collected unemployment. To satisfy his chief passion he bought odds and ends of clothes in charity shops and second-hand stores. Dressing up cost him virtually nothing, but occasionally he'd see something that he just had to have—some item of clothing he couldn't live without. He was like a starving artist who needs that one tube of paint to complete his masterpiece.

Around this time he met up with another inspirational model like Philip Salon. His name was Martin Degville, and he looked like an albino James Dean. Degville had a superb bleached "quiff" that rolled over the crown of his head like high tide at Waikiki. He also had a downy white mustache that, unlike George's, grew naturally rather than from the lead of a drawing pencil.

The two hit it off at once; Degville lived for "dressing up" as he did, and Degville could be very inspired, providing George with the stimulation he needed to become "really loony."

But Degville also had a serious interest in clothing. He wanted to go into the design business; Birmingham, a couple of hours' drive from London in England's Midlands, was the place where he chose to launch his career. He asked George to go up there with him, and since there was nothing George liked more than clothes, he readily accepted. Altogether he spent a year in Birmingham, completing there, so to speak, his undergraduate degree in "weirdness."

The streets of this grimy, industrial city had never seen anything like the "ugly sisters," as George called the twosome he made with Martin. They competed as to who could "out-dress" the other. It was good fun and instructive, leading to endless experimentation on George's part. In the end he painted his face green and his neck red and dyed his hair purple, plaiting it in various places in anticipation of his later "dredlocks."

He and Martin shared an apartment with a couple of girls who continually found their inspiration in the boys' hair and dress styles. It was a hectic life. During the day George helped out in the clothing stall Martin had opened in a Birmingham market. At night there were parties, clubs, concerts and outings, all of which required hours of preening before mirrors. Tirelessly the "ugly sisters" girded on heaps of clothes, cast them off and, giggling madly, tried on others until either one or the other was voted looking the most "weird."

It was in Birmingham, under Degville's inspiration, that George began wearing dresses and makeup with the consciousness that they were the real expression of the "being different."

When George O'Dowd returned to London, the seventies were drawing to a close and it seemed that the times were gasping for a breath of fresh air. A novel group of young rebels had come to the fore who called themselves New Romantics. They saw themselves in revolt against the punks and Teds, a revolt that took place on the streets with weapons consisting of tassels and flounces and colorful silky things.

In attitude, the New Romantics were closer to the hippies of the sixties than punks or Teds, but their clothes were far more elaborate than the careless fashions from the psychedelic past. The New Romantics had a passion for the clothes of bygone days, favoring taffetta vests and silk pantaloons, crepe dresses, tasseled belts and hooded gowns. Their style was bizarre and extravagant; as one London tabloid defined it, "Anything goes as long as it is over the top and helps to bring out a pantomime fantasy of the past."

The tabloid might have been describing George, as after Degville and Birmingham, he was well "over the top." A seventeen-year-old boy who wears makeup and dresses and has purple spiky hair is bound to get noticed, and it did not take long for the garish British press to discover the most outrageous "personality" that had come along in a very long time. The boy who used white face powder, lipstick and rouge, parading the streets and visiting the clubs in the most unbelievable outfits, was at first thought of as the flagship of the New Romantics, which George O'Dowd was always at pains to disavow. He was not a "stupid New Romantic"; he didn't belong to this or that movement. He was absolutely original, in a class of his own.

Photographs of him began appearing in many magazines and people could not help but be startled and take notice. At first the readers were confused, not knowing whether he was a boy or a girl, but when it became well-established that beneath the makeup and the ribbons there was a seventeen-year-old boy, his name was made. He became a mild sensation, a minor media event, often ridiculed, derided and laughed at, but not forgotten.

To his own family it was incomprehensible. His father couldn't understand it at all. He thought his son had become the leader of a movement. New Romantics sounded ominous, something like the Socialist Party. He failed to see why magazines would want to run pictures of someone who looked so odd, and he could not understand how George could be proud of exhibiting himself like that to millions of people. George's mother, however, understood him better, and she began to help him by sewing his dresses and making suggestions about fabrics and designs. She was pleased when turning the pages of the *Sun* or *Mirror* she'd see George modeling a fashion she'd helped create.

George O'Dowd became known as a "gender bender." But he explained it was not quite so simple, telling reporters, "I don't feel very feminine at all. I think in pictures I may be very feminine, but in real life I am quite a masculine guy." Another time he said that he was not really aware of his sexual identity and that with makeup he was "just accentuating his features" to make himself "look more attractive." With every picture in the paper the subject of his sexuality was rehashed. George himself never tired of discussing it because that was his mystery—he did not care if people thought he was a girl, because that speculation only deepened the mystery.

He had taken a leaf from a "mad guy" he'd seen in Oxford Street. This person walked up and down with a sandwich board bearing the nonsensical legend, "Sitting, peanuts, lentils." He'd been there for years and everyone knew him. That crazy person was a "face"; he was a character because he put himself out. The guy with the sign was his "own medium," so to speak. George got the message. What was important was that people were talking about him.

When you were being talked about you were a "celebrity." A celebrity had to be constantly doing something, he had to be constantly original, and so for George every day became a new adventure.

One day he would show up at a club wearing a toga-like dress with his hair bleached white and standing straight on end like icicles. A few days later he would be in an outfit resembling that of Emperor Ming in "Captain Video"—a vinyl top with enormous shoulders. On another night it would be a modified gladiator's tunic that looked like a leftover from a Cecille B. DeMille spectacular. He drew a lot of comment with his nun's habit, complete with wooden crucifix ("a present from the Vatican," he said) and Kung Fu slippers ("from a Chinese supermarket"). The face that looked out demurely from under the nun's headdress was elaborately made up, with huge dracula-like eyebrows, thick green eyeliner and ruby-red lips.

As the toast of photographers, with his pictures constantly in the newspapers, George became the classic example of the celebrity who had never actually *done* anything. Yet by his own account, he was leading a glamorous life. He had no money, no job, no responsibilities. He'd get up at four in the afternoon and go to bed at four in the morning. He spent hours in front of the mirror and almost as much time choosing what to wear, and when he went out on the street people laughed.

A few years hence, from the height of his fame, he would

always remember what it felt like "to be treated almost like a clown." Yet if people asked why he wanted to look the way he did, he couldn't give a clear answer.

"It's like trying to give an explanation for sleeping and eating," he'd say; it was something completely natural, a part of his being. What he wore was "basically normal." His makeup was "something really personal." It was not a question of sex, either; sex had never been an "obsession"; it was "just like eating a bag of crisps." He gave a million explanations, but in the end it boiled down to one thing— he didn't particularly want to look normal. He didn't particularly want to look like George O'Dowd from Shooters Hill.

"Sometimes," he said, "you just sit at the mirror and think, 'I hate you,' so you just change it."

5

"Face-About-Town"

As a budding "celebrity," George O'Dowd had achieved one goal, he had broken free from the bonds of the working class; he would not be trapped in the building trade, or any other dead-end job, nor would he spend his life in a tiny house on a depressing street, in a colorless existence stalked by boredom. He had avoided "boring" business suits and could dress up any way he pleased. He was leading the only life he desired, that of a social butterfly with gaudy painted wings.

In this busy life around town he soon saw how people looked up to him because they felt the power of his "personality"; they admired him because he broke the rules and flew straight in the face of convention; whatever he said carried conviction because everybody understood their own hypocrisies; Boy George flamboyantly lived the life he had chosen.

His life attracted attention; the attention was satisfying to his ego, yet with all the gossip and all the fascination he stirred up everywhere, he was still left with the necessity of making a living. He was still living in abandoned buildings or with friends. He had started out unconcerned about money because he'd always felt that he could achieve anything. But after having become a "minor celebrity," he said to himself, "Okay, I want to do something now." He decided that he wanted a career, something he could enjoy. What he enjoyed was "dressing up," so he began to think about modeling.

As a "Face-About-Town," a "poser" on the club scene, he knew hundreds of people. He was in constant contact with people who set the trends. It was a world where "decadence" was not a word of opprobrium. The club scene mirrored society, for society followed where it led, and George was welcomed in this world because he was more "outrageous" than any of the "trend-setters." It was not difficult for him to make a little money here and there, or to find people who liked to do him favors.

Being established as a "Face-About-Town," it was not difficult to find modeling jobs. He began working for the Peter Benison Agency, which wanted "weirdos" to model in advertising. The agency was looking for models who "live the part they play." George got a number of bookings, among them one for British Airways. Then he landed a job for a few days with the Royal Shakespeare Company through his friend Mad Jean, with whom he was living on Goodge Street. The RSC was putting on a production of "Naked Robots," and Boy George became their "stylist" to give the play an authentic "punk look."

To do the costuming for "Naked Robots," George turned to a clothes shop called the Regal. George, being always fully costumed himself, impressed the owner of the shop,

Peter Small, who was connected with an institution known as the Street Theatre; and when the job with the RSC ended, George stayed on at the Regal as a window dresser. Being on display in the window while arranging costumes in artful compositions was something he enjoyed, but it was not a "career."

George had always been able to charm people. He was vivacious, and his vivacity was infectious. He was humorous, and even when his humor turned sharp it still had a kind of mad charm.

People took to him because fending for himself on the streets he'd learned how to use his charm well. He did not conceal himself; he spontaneously exposed his weak points and strong. But he was always aware of the "effect." Whether or not people thought of him as a "poof," or a "weirdo," he was always able to convert them to assist him. He could befriend people, men as well as women, and inspire them to work on his behalf. And Peter Small, not long after hiring him as a window dresser, set him up in a shop of his own to produce "imaginative" clothing ideas with another designer, Sue Clowes.

The shop was called The Foundry. It was just off Carnaby Street and it was to be significant for the career that was to change George O'Dowd into Boy George of Culture Club.

The theme of the fabrics produced by The Foundry was described as a combination of Religion, History, War and Sacred Figures. The symbols it used included icons, the cross and the Star of David, along with Hebrew lettering. The idea of the designs was the "cultural mix we enjoy," and the idea stuck with George when he came to name the band which was to bring him world renown and make him into a *true* celebrity; that is, a celebrity who had done something.

Sue Clowes was a few years older than George. She had

studied textile design and run a successful dress stall in a London market. George liked her fabric prints, but was not very impressed with her dress designs. When it came to designing women's clothes, he had his own ideas. That the public was not ready for the combined Clowes-George onslaught on fashion could be gathered from some of the negative reactions printed in the newspaper columns.

Sue Clowes would go on to cut a fashion name for herself after Culture Club went Number One and everyone wanted to look like Boy George. She helped dress Boy George and Culture Club, designing their ambiguous costumes, giving them the symbolic "cultural" clutter, but after a while her relationship with George became strained. George allowed no one to tamper with his "personality," and that included Sue Clowes. He knew exactly how he wanted to dress; it was a subject to which he devoted most of his waking time.

While he was with The Foundry, however, he enjoyed himself, and he did not leave the shop until Culture Club got off the drawing board and he became Boy George. At The Foundry, with the facilities of a designer, a shop and unlimited possibilities to be original, George was able to indulge himself thoroughly. He could design clothes for himself, model them and see himself in the fashion pages of newspapers and magazines. Modeling had been a passion of his ever since his first professional exposure at fifteen in a hairdressers' magazine, showing a surprisingly clean-cut boy with a normal head of hair.

"George O'Dowd, nineteen," reads the caption of one newspaper fashion photograph titled "Flamboyant." It shows him smiling, slimmer than the current Boy George, hands on hips, wearing leg warmers and a black crepe twenties dress with beads, tassels and a dashing scarf around the neck to hide its thickness. Under the dress George wears old school trousers which the article says "he tapered himself," and Chinese slippers beneath the leg warmers. The "crimpled blouse" over which the dress is draped, the caption reads, he got "from his mum"; the outfit was rounded off by a "black felt hat and assorted earrings."

6

Lieutenant Lush

George O'Dowd had always been determined to be "on top." He considered it his job to make people aware of him—if someone had come along looking as he did, it would have been his "job" to be more outrageous. By going about like an extraterrestrial he had succeeded in coining his "curiosity value." But as a designer in The Foundry he'd also helped start a trend in far-out and ambiguous fashions, and since in England the world of fashion and music are closely allied, it was inevitable that he'd get involved in music. It was no longer enough simply to be known for being "weird." He was no longer satisfied with being a "Face-About-Town," a "freak mode." He wanted to be a "pop star."

To become a "pop star" is the dream of every British youngster. They dream of it as American kids dream of Hollywood. The dream is especially strong among English working-class kids for whom most avenues of advancement are closed. The dream began with the Beatles, and for the current generation the dream is maintained by the tremendous explosion of new bands that has enabled London to remain the rock capital of the world.

In the mid-seventies the British rock scene was as dull as that in the U.S. Then came punk, and suddenly a thousand bands, clubs and discos bloomed. The punk sound reinforced the belief that anyone can start a band. It started with the Sex Pistols, and the energy of the early punk bands like them created the wave of new groups that dominate the charts today—bands like the Clash, the Fixx, Duran Duran, the Police, the Eurythmics, Madness, The Human League, Def Lepard and the most phenomenal success of them all, Culture Club.

Early punk groups, such as the Sex Pistols and the Clash, went back to rock's primitive roots. They threw studio polish and technical experience out the window, going in for raw power, ideas and personality. In England the record companies quickly picked up on the sounds. After discovering the committed following of fans that many of the new groups rolled up, they threw open their doors to creative new ideas; and that in turn returned the feeling among young music-makers that anyone could make a record. As a result, one new band after another could be seen setting a trend that spread from London across Europe and the Atlantic.

George was living in the midst of this musical excitement because rock stars, trends and fashions came largely out of the clubs where he hung out. He was a fixture at places like the Blitz, a bleak, freaky, cradle of punk and "beyond-punk." He spent a lot of time at Billy's, a club where the New Romanticism started. He was on the scene with the likes of Duran Duran, which was too "clean-cut" for his liking, and Spandau Ballet, which was too "intellectual," mixing politics with music, the sort of thing he didn't care for in the least. His friend Jeremiah Healey, of Haysi Fantayzee, for a while was a strong influence on him.

He saw a lot of people getting bands together. Some of the bands he liked, others he hated, but he noticed that practically none of them had anything like a "personality." He also thought that none of the singers he heard could sing as well as he did, even though he'd never really sung before except as a "lark." That gave him the idea of starting his first band in the abandoned building where he was living.

He called the group In Praise of Lemmings. It had a drummer called Luke, a guitarist by the name of Johnny Suede, and a bass player by the name of Kirk Brandon, who would later attempt a most baleful brand of punk in his Theatre of Hate.

The band rehearsed industriously and George was happy to be singing. But it soon dawned on him that the band was going nowhere. It had no identity, no personality and no ideas. It espoused the ethic of the post-punk bands, an ethic he despised, "the idea of trying not to learn too much about the music because it might take the 'feel' away." A lot of punk bands were like that, started by people who wanted to be rock stars by playing non-melodic, unpolished, ugly music.

"It was a real shambles," Boy George says, "very much like a dirge. The music was very kind of political, very heavy, very sexual, the words were very Jean Cocteau."

But when the group split up he was at a loss, not quite knowing what to do with the instrument that was his voice. He knew he could sing but he did not know how or in what "direction" to develop this talent. Thus far he only knew

51

what he didn't want to be. He didn't want to be another David Bowie or Roxy Music's Bryan Ferry, "another great white hope with an angular voice going 'Ooh-woo-woo' in an affected way." He also discovered that what he disliked about punk rock was its lack of "quality"—it was "all young people with problems, locking themselves up in their bedroom with tennis rackets." He had never been a student, but the music sounded to him very "studenty"—like the Spandau Ballet, which was trying hard to be both musical and "heady."

His tastes in music were actually more conservative, and also more eclectic. He had started out liking musicals such as "The King and I," "South Pacific" and "The Sound of Music." He'd grown up on American rock, and his favorites were people like Gladys Knight and Stevie Wonder. He also liked Rod Stewart, Marvin Gaye and especially the Philadelphia soul of Smokey Robinson. These performers influenced him because all of them had distinctive voices and they spoke soulfully to the emotions, and that soulful emotionalism was the quality he detected in his own voice.

He had discovered the clear smooth beauty of his voice at parties, when he used to get up and sing. Through the din and smoke he would listen to the crooning sound that seemed, like everything about him, very special. Singing was another way of being different. The words of the songs were like the makeup he used that made him more attractive to himself. When he sang he felt more acceptable. But singing was also something very private. He could express his true emotions in song.

In the early part of 1980, George was still living in his abandoned building, designing at The Foundry, dressing the windows for Peter Small and modeling for the Peter Benison

Agency. The girl doing the booking for the agency had a boyfriend named Matthew Ashland, a guitarist for a group called BowWowWow. George and this couple became good friends; George would go around to their flat a lot, "pissing about, singing old jazz songs."

Ashland was impressed by George's singing; they'd get together and go through some jazz tunes and Ashland would be surprised by the power and range of George's voice. He suggested that George try out for BowWowWow; the group was auditioning for a lead vocalist, and one night at one of the clubs, George—dressed in a straw hat and tottering drunkenly—went to see the manager of BowWowWow, Malcolm McLaren. He learned from McLaren that the group's current lead singer, Annabella, had been a "last resort," that originally they had wanted a "sort of bronzed Adonis type but very effeminate." George figured from the start that he was not right for the role.

Malcolm McLaren was known as the hottest promoter of new bands in England. He had been a prime mover of the punk sound, making a big splash with Johnny Rotten of the Sex Pistols. He was a changeable jack-of-all-trades on the rock scene, having managed the New York Dolls and Adam Ant, and being as well a performer in his own right. All these successes, however, had earned him chiefly notoriety and the reputation of an "exploiter" who manipulated people, the media and record companies.

Music promoters like Malcolm McLaren would find it hard to function in the American record industry, which is structured on corporate lines where to fail is a disgrace, the fear of which often deters innovation. The industry is interested in music, but sometimes afraid of the new. For a new performer it is therefore almost impossible to break in, whereas in England, where the business is altogether freewheeling, almost to the point of chaos, the new is easy to sell. Most of it is "gimmicky"; a band may have a hit and never be heard from again, but in all the British effervescence of sound an occasional bubble will swell into a wave. The Beatles were one example; Culture Club is another.

Malcolm McLaren was constantly looking for new ideas. When punk came around, he professed to have pagan, anarchic beliefs—rock 'n roll then meant to him "sex, subversion and style." While promoting the punk sound, he came up with Johnny Rotten (who was called that because his teeth were bad) and Sid Vicious (who was accused in New York of murdering his girl friend, but O.D.'d before coming to trial).

For BowWowWow, McLaren became a New Romantic, and he was grooming the band's lead singer, a fifteen-year-old named Annabella Lwin, into the star of the movement. Unfortunately, Annabella seemed both "uppity" and wavering in her commitment to BowWowWow, which as a group was actually quite successful and at the peak of London trendiness. All of Annabella's musical experience had consisted of watching the "Top of the Pops" on television. She was a fair singer, but she lacked drive. The lure of fame didn't seem to mean much to her.

At the time Boy George auditioned for BowWowWow, he was unaware that his try-out was merely a ploy McLaren was using to get Annabella to shape up. McLaren was hoping that the threat of her replacement by someone as outrageous as George would make her serious about BowWowWow.

Boy George was not happy with his audition. He felt that the band hated him because of the way he looked. His years of testing people's reactions to him enabled him to tell when people disliked him; he felt sure the band members thought him an idiot. They demanded that he learn the song "W.O.R.K.," as Boy George recalls it, "in ten seconds." The band members didn't like his audition; they thought he was "really camp."

But McLaren approved; it was good enough, and after another try-out he put Boy George in front of three thousand people at the Rainbow Theatre in London. McLaren did not care much how well he performed; he was going to fire him, anyway, after Annabella had been a little frightened and decided to buck up.

In his first performance ever, George O'Dowd walked out on the stage and sang an old rockabilly song by Peanuts Wilson, "Cast Iron Arm." His appearance came as a surprise to a lot of people who didn't know he could sing. The audience responded favorably and he got some good reviews, too.

Everyone in the audience thought he was a girl, a very striking girl, incredibly made up, though with a pleasant breathy voice. But the three thousand people had come to see Annabella. It was hard for George to accept second string, especially to Annabella, who had "visions of herself as an air hostess or a waitress in a delicatessen," he complained.

McLaren was obsessed with the idea that he could turn Annabella into a "sexy little Lolita of the eighties." A "Lolita," someone young and naive like Annabella, was not George's kind of woman; he liked Dolly Parton because she was almost a parody of a woman, and he liked Liz Taylor because she seemed to always get what she wanted, which was something really fine and womanly.

Rumors abounded in the press. Would George replace Annabella? But McLaren had his fixation with her. He could not abandon her because she was an "idea." There was a

New Romantic movement. Annabella, with her mysterious gypsy look, was perfect to lead it. George had a very nice voice; he was amusing and intelligent and sexy, and that was all McLaren saw. He was puzzled by George's funny side. He did not see him as George saw himself, as a unique person who could sing. McLaren thought George "a bit odd" and believed that he just wouldn't "go."

Nevertheless, the rumors continued. One report said George was going to sign with RCA. Then another said he and Annabella were going on a big tour of Europe. McLaren had created a new name for George, "Lieutenant Lush." True to this image, George was going to sing and dance in a certain way. BowWowWow was finished being New Romantic; it was going to be a kind of Motown revue band backing up Boy George and Annabella, with a couple of other dancers and lots of lively action. Posters were being put up everywhere for BowWowWow with Annabella and featuring Lieutenant Lush. But after three months' rehearsals, McLaren suddenly canceled the idea. He still refused to give up on Annabella, but he promised George that he was going to put together a whole new band just for Lieutenant Lush.

At that point George exploded, "This is bullocks! I'm leaving." He realized that McLaren had been stringing him along, though he was not altogether displeased to be leaving. He and Annabella had been struggling for the spotlight on stage, and George felt he could no longer handle that.

The experience was a bitter pill. But by now he was obsessed.

"I can't *stand* this anymore," he thought, "I wanna be in a *band*. I wanna sing."

Boy George

ALAN KLEINBERG

Hello, world!

ALAN KLEINBERG

In a mood

On the doorstep

Will I be a star?

Making the magic happen

Star at work

Spellbinder

High stepping

On stage with Helen Terry

With Erin Moran of HAPPY DAYS

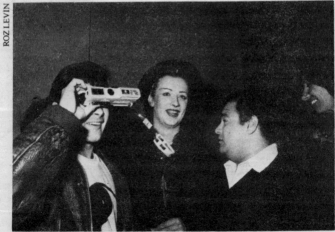

With Jon Moss and Frank M. Dileo

With Steve Winwood

Boy George celebrates his arrival in America
with Susan Blond, vice president of Epic Records

With Jon Moss

Lonely life of a star

At home

Modeling for a
hair-style magazine

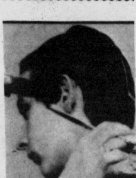

Hair-style model

HEY SUSAN!
GET OFF
MY PHOTO!

Self-portrait done for Susan Blond,
vice president of Epic Records

Culture Club. Left to right: Jon Moss, Roy Hay, Mickey Craig

With Jon Moss: thoughtful

At home with Culture Club. Left to right:
Jon Moss, Roy Hay, Mickey Craig

Left to right: Jon Moss, Roy Hay, Mickey Craig

Rewards of fame

7

Almost

a Star

Though the experience with BowWowWow had been a disappointment, it led to a result that by now had become routine in Boy George's life. He got attention. But this time it was not on the "kooky page" of the tabloids. Through his association with McLaren he received much mention in the musical trade papers. Again, the interest at first concerned mainly his "curiosity value." There had never been a singer who had dared go on stage quite the way he looked; a fresh buzz of gossip sprang up, and, as usual, the publicity proved helpful.

One day he received a phone call from someone who introduced himself as Ashley Goodall from EMI, the big record company. He suggested that they have a meeting.

"What about?" Boy George asked naively.

"Well, you're a singer now, aren't you?" Goodall said.

"Not now, I'm not in a band."

"Well, you could be a solo artist," Goodall proposed.

It was a free meal, something Boy George could ill afford to pass up in those days, so he went to the meeting, where Goodall was very nice, saying that he could make him into a "big star."

Boy George thought about it and for a long time he couldn't make up his mind. He'd been around music and bands long enough to see the snares that entrapped many who, like him, had been offered a lot of money and either vanished after a song or two or failed miserably from the start. He'd seen it happen to Steve Strange, his friend from Billy's. Just recently he'd seen his friend Kirk Brandon's Theatre of Hate go under beneath their own punk rock blasts because it had been the wrong thing at the time. He'd seen most of the people associated with the early "star system," such as Gary Glitter, fade out of this system that was supposed to ensure their eternal existence. He'd also seen a lot of people who had worked very hard end up not making a penny because they had signed bad contracts and made a lot of mistakes. The whole punk movement and the New Romantic wave, apart from frightening a few adults, ultimately hadn't amounted to much. He'd seen all these people play it the wrong way and he finally concluded that it would be wrong for him to take Goodall up on his offer. Goodall, without even knowing whether he could sing, was obviously thinking only of "packaging" the outrageous aspect of him; as a solo, George realized, he would be just an exploited product.

He decided to follow his instincts. His instincts told him that with no musical training and hardly any experience his solo career would not turn out well; he would merely be a singing "weirdo." What he needed was to grow with a band of his own. He had lots of ideas, but they were scattered; he needed to concentrate them by singing with a group that could jell together so it would be able to create something distinctive that was not "packaged" in production-line fashion.

The band he wanted was now about to become a reality, and it would fulfill his hopes in a way that even in his fondest dreams he could have hardly imagined.

Goodall was not the only person to be struck by the news and pictures of Lieutenant Lush in the trade papers. Across town, in Hammersmith, very much on the "other side of the tracks," Mikey Craig, a twenty-year-old English-born Jamaican with a fearsome Mohican atop an otherwise gentle face, was studying a picture of George and Annabella in the *New Musical Express*. His initial reaction to the photo was like that of many others who saw George for the first time, whether in a photograph or in the flesh.

"Good God," Mikey Craig said to himself. Then he said, "Hmmmm, I *must* find out more."

Craig was a bassist and looking for work. Like George, he'd been knocking about the streets and hanging about clubs since he was thirteen. His passion then had also been "dressing up," but an even greater passion was dancing. He came from a neat, God-fearing, working-class home. His parents had hopes to see him go into a profession. In this respect their son was to disappoint them. The school he was attending had the atmosphere of a prison-house, and as soon as Mikey turned fifteen he gladly escaped its stifling confinement, giving himself up completely to his dancing passion. He didn't play an instrument until after he got a job as DJ at a club in Soho. At sixteen, almost casually, he got hold of a bass guitar. He learned by playing along with records—funky, Motown, blues, rock, but mostly reggae. Bob Marley early became his favorite.

At sixteen, Craig kept up on the bass guitar while doing odd jobs such as road building. Then he landed a job in a sound studio, starting off as a tap op and working his way up to editing and other tasks. He began jamming while living in Bristol, where he stayed two years. The people he jammed with were "long-haired hippies," but they were also good musicians and he learned quickly. By 1980, having returned to London, he felt he had paid his apprentice dues and was ready to form a band. Seeing the picture of George in the paper, he also saw an "opportunity" after reading that McLaren was thinking of forming a band around the singer. He checked around with some friends who knew McLaren and it was arranged that he'd be able to find George at a place called Planets on Piccadilly.

Mikey had no trouble picking out George when a few days later he walked into the club. He went up to him and said, "I've seen your picture in the *NME*. I wanna be in a band with you."

"Simple as that?" George said.

"Yeah, I'm a bass player."

George said he'd like to form a band but that McLaren would not be involved. That was all right with Craig. They had several discussions afterward. Neither had much experience, but one thing they shared was that they were desperately anxious to get on with it and have a real band. George then found a guitar player, Johnny Suede, from his old band In Praise of Lemmings. They then sat around and worked out a name, The Sex Gang Children, demonstrating that George had not fully freed himself from Kirk Brandon, the punk messiah from Theatre of Hate, and that the influence of the Blitz scene was still not completely shaken off.

Someone George knew had the telephone number of a drummer named Jon Moss. Kirk Brandon knew him. George had seen Moss around the King's Road. Moss was someone he vaguely knew about as having played in some successful punk bands.

George had met loads of drummers before and all he knew was that they were "the most obnoxious breed." But, overcoming his misgivings, he called Moss, rapping in his usual mile-a-minute fashion. When he mentioned Bow-WowWow, Moss got interested. A rehearsal meeting was arranged.

And it worked. It worked marvelously well, in fact, because one of the "obnoxious drummer breed" proved to be the crucial element to give the band the discipline, control and direction it very much needed. The first thing Jon Moss said to George was, "I don't like that name; I'm not playing in a band called The Sex Gang Children." George and Mikey had written a song called "Mask." Jon thought it was horrible. He thought the band was horrible. But the voice stood out. He realized right away it was "brilliant."

Today it would seem that Culture Club's success has been rapid, sudden and instantaneous. Two years ago there was no band by that name and apart from England, where tabloid readers knew of a George O'Dowd who was shameless and dressed shockingly, no one had heard of him. Boy George's meteoric rise to stardom would therefore tend to support all those beliefs the public maintains concerning "luck," getting the "right breaks" or knowing the "right people." All these elements *do* play a part in success, but they play a much smaller part than is generally supposed. Talent, discipline, organization, hard work and determination are the things that really matter. Jon Moss came from

61

a different background than the working-class George O'Dowd and Mikey Craig. Also, compared to them, he was musically an "old pro." Moss realized that, apart from the talent, George and Mikey were lacking the necessary qualities for success, qualities which are rarely fostered by life on the streets—they had no discipline and little capacity for organization and sustained hard work.

Jon Moss' background was middle-class, well-to-do, Jewish and proper. He was twenty-five years old and when he met George for that first rehearsal in March 1981, he had already gone through a period of trying to find himself. As a youngster with defiantly long hair, he had attended a private school where he had gone in heavily for sports, particularly boxing. His parents had wanted him to go on to college, but, restless and unfocused, he showed little spirit for continuing his academic career. At sixteen, he had a spell in his father's clothing store in the West End. Unable to bear it, he left after a few months. He next went through a series of brief careers, working as a salesman, as an apprentice printer and with a music agency. Then came a sustained involvement in bands, which left him exhausted and disenchanted, so that with his last money he paid for a weekend consciousness-raising seminar, hoping to find some answers but instead, as he recalls, going briefly "mad."

Jon had been playing drums since the age of fourteen, absorbing a wide range of influences, mostly pop, jazz and rock, from The Searchers and Freddy and the Dreamers to the Beatles and King Crimson, from Led Zeppelin and Spirit to Sly and The Family Stone. His tastes were eclectic and unformed. He'd also made various attempts at starting bands, a whole series of them with kooky names like Phone Bone Boulevard, Pastrami Barmy and Eskimo Norbert.

The first time he linked up with a better-known band came as the result of answering a blind ad which landed him a gig with the Clash, which had just then recorded "White Riot." He played with them for three months before they made any singles or did any shows. He did a small art film with them and some recording that was never released. Though he loved their music, he didn't like their "stance," a lot of political "sloganeering" which seemed empty to him, with little relation to music. He ended up arguing with them and finally he left.

For the next three years, Jon got to know the side of band life which eventually led to his disenchantment. He spent much of these years touring, wearing a black outfit and living like a rock 'n roller. After a brief tour with the Stranglers, a frenetic period followed—he joined The Damned and it was all booze and fighting. He'd get into the mini-bus with The Damned in the early morning along with a crate of lager—all "very rock 'n roll and let's all kill ourselves before we're too old." Then one night they went a bit too far, and when he came out he thought, "Why did I do that?" He left The Damned and formed a group called The Edge; their sound was "punky" but the musicianship was good, and eventually The Edge ended up as a house band at Stiff Records. They became so much of a session band that he became dulled by the routine. He played a brief stint with Adam Ant, but received no credit for his contribution to Ant's "Dirk Wears White Socks" album. He got an invitation to join the Ramones but turned it down.

He had become stale and bored. He no longer wanted to be just another drummer, mechanically laying one roll on top of another. He wanted to play music that was creative, inventive, adventurous, sparkling. He'd been in a lot of bands and hadn't made much headway. He'd learned the unromantic side of rock 'n roll—that many people in bands didn't really want to do anything unless it was destructive.

* * *

When Moss received the call from George inviting him to the rehearsal, he listened to the high-pitched, slightly frantic, rapid-fire voice, and he was prepared. He knew about the "Blitz kids," as the outrageous young patrons of that particular club in London were known, and he knew Kirk Brandon, George's sidekick, who looked like a cross between a wraith and a punk. Brandon was at that first meeting, faithfully at George's side.

"Well, what do you want me to do?" Jon asked, after having listened to the dreadful song called "Mask."

"I don't know," George said. "Well, what I'm telling you is that I want to start a band. I don't want you to come and play drums *for* me, I want you to start a band *with* me."

"Okay, that's a good idea."

George was abrim with enthusiasm. "Yeah, it's great. I want you all to start a band *with* me. I don't know what I want to play and I don't care but I don't want a set idea."

The music was awful. George, Mikey and Johnny Suede had no experience. It was a crazy scene, Jon thought, but there was something about it—vibrant, tingling, alive. They weren't cynical. They could work and have fun too. And he thought, "This is just what I'm looking for." He realized that they needed him and he needed them.

8

Culture Club

Moss had been playing rock for eight years and had gotten as far as he wanted to go. As an experienced musician, he realized after meeting George that there wasn't really a band. But he saw potential. Moss knew what he wanted. He realized there were great possibilities.

They didn't know what they wanted to do, but Jon wanted the band to be a commercial band. He didn't want to play punk or post-punk, heavy metal, disco, funky, New Romantic, acid-rock or any of the latest trends. He wanted to go back to basics. He wanted to be in a band that sold millions of records. He wanted to play songs that would be liked by his grandfather as well as by his baby sister, songs that were warm, tuneful, colorful and danceable. No politics, no protest, no new wave but natural, melodic music with good vocals and good vibes. Pop, pure and simple.

George quite agreed. He liked the traditional—Gene Pitney, Dolly Parton, Stevie Wonder, R&B, soul. It was thumbs down on David Bowie, McLaren, Donna Summer. He agreed with Jon. Back to basics. Millions of records. Romance, love, pop.

George had at first been a little wary of Moss' experience. He himself didn't have any to speak of. He couldn't read music—he couldn't play a lottery ticket. But he had ideas and he had melodies. Melodies came out of his head—his head was bursting with melodies—and lyrics just bubbled up naturally from an inexhaustible, though not always comprehensible, verbal fountain. What he needed was someone to whom he could sing his melodies and who would translate them into chords and arrangements. So at first he had been worried that Jon, with his greater experience, would cramp his style. He laid down the rule that "everybody would put their ideas in."

There would be no set ideas, no fixed sound. None of them knew how to write songs, and they were to learn together, writing good songs about love that everybody could understand. Jon proved that he had the right attitude about all of this, but he was adamant that two things needed to be changed, the name, The Sex Gang Children, and the guitarist, Johnny Suede.

Johnny Suede had been around George since the old days at the abandoned building, helping produce the shambles that was In Praise of Lemmings.

"I can't sack him," George said.

"Okay," said Jon, "I'll sack him."

Johnny Suede took it well and departed with good grace. The final member of the band, Roy Hay, came on board shortly afterwards. George and Jon had been listening to a lot of guitarists. In fact, on the day Hay showed up, they

66

were actually waiting to listen to someone from a group called Basement 5 who didn't make it. As Hay had already auditioned, George decided, "I'm gonna keep him."

What he liked about Hay was his complete devotion to playing good guitar. Hay was interested in nice chords and not at all in anything that was "happening." He was not part of any "scene." The band's final member, having overcome his first astonishment at George's mascara, flounces and ribbons, laconically observed to himself, "We may not sell a lot of records, but we'll get a lot of attention."

Roy Hay, as a not-yet twenty-year-old, a very respectable former insurance clerk and hairdresser from suburban Essex, rounded out the ethnic composition of the band. As Boy George would some time later put it, "Roy is kind of very White. He adds the straight classical side to Culture Club." Mikey was black, George was Irish Catholic, Jon was Jewish. This mix was further complicated by the fact that each member had his musical preferences: Mikey was basically a reggae bassist; Jon was eclectic, with a proclivity towards jazz, Latin American and African music; Roy Hay leaned more to the rock side of things, with a long-time passion for Steely Dan; and George was into R&B, and especially soul.

They were all different people with different tastes. They were black and white, and they were from different cultural backgrounds. Together they would produce one good, hummable, danceable, commercial sound. This mixed facet of the group solved the problem of the other change Jon wanted to make. For their new name, an alternative to The Sex Gang Children, George had in mind something simple; he didn't want something "arty" like Spandau Ballet. He suggested Caravan, a name with a traveling connotation. The question hung fire for a brief while. Then Jon one day was talking to Mikey about how London was full of different cultures—and the name naturally suggested itself. To George the name appeared a projection of the kind of design theme he had introduced with Susan Clowes at The Foundry.

It was decided the name would be Culture Club, and thus the commercial music phenomenon of the eighties was born.

9

White Boy

The Culture Club sound that is heard today, the slick machine-tooled new-wave bubblegum, is a far cry from the jagged sound the band ground out when it began rehearsing in the summer of '81. At that point, George had not yet found a distinctive vocal style; basically he was still learning to sing by copying the singers he admired; it was frustrating, and frequently he'd say to Jon, "Oh, we should give up."

But Jon would insist, "You're a really good singer." And they'd try again.

During that early summer and fall, it was Jon Moss who held the band together. Roy was the most musical member, serious about his craft, dogged, solid, painstaking, continually exploring new arrangements he could put his guitar into. Mikey was adept and quick, but easily distracted. George frankly recalls those trying days and the strength

Jon imparted to keep the group going: "Myself and Mikey were very lazy, although Mikey wouldn't probably admit that. But I *know* that we were like a pair of slobs. Y'know, it was like 'Oh, we'll do it next week, the week after...' but Jon had been in bands for eight years and he wanted to get on with it. He'd say, 'I don't want to mess about; I'm not taking all this garbage.'"

Moss persisted. He and George had grown very close. Moss saw in George what McLaren had been unable to fathom. McLaren, too, had recognized that George had a great voice. But he'd been unable to figure out what to do with George himself; he'd tried to create a character, Lieutenant Lush, and it hadn't worked. Moss saw that the character need not be created; that, in fact, the character was already there, being none other than George O'Dowd himself, the outrageous boy-girl with the high-speed "motor mouth" that never stopped to take a breath, that poured forth a ceaseless "rap" that contradicted itself a million times but that, because of the mere flow of words, the energy, gave the appearance of a seamless web.

Culture Club's drummer had seen bands come and go; he'd seen them go under not because of their musicianship, which was often very good, but because they lacked "personality." The Beatles had it; so did the Rolling Stones. George O'Dowd, Moss recognized, had it, and by extension, Culture Club would have it. Moss saw George as a showman. George saw himself this way too. "I'm interested in being a personality," he'd always said; he'd been working on it all his life. And, like Moss, he knew instinctively that "to get people's attention you have to be more than a musician."

However, before George could unfold this "personality," the band had to improve its musicianship and it had to come up with songs.

It was very clear from the beginning that they would not be a fusion band associated with one particular sound; for that their tastes were too unformed. Nor would they be anything like the earlier experimental British bands to whom music often meant making a musical statement. They wanted to be a pop group, a commercial band that sold records and made money. They knew what had been successful in the past, and they were able to capture this formula musically because of George's facility in coming up with melodic tunes, which he either dreamed up himself or, more often, modified from an old favorite.

To write songs you need three things: melody, rhythm and music. George *did* know how to come up with a melody; they sprang from some mechanism of his brain like a music box where all the songs he'd ever heard lay stored. The box shook, and out "popped" the tune. So Moss devised a system that turned out to be extremely workable. Whenever George got "inspired," he would sing the melody to Jon, who then, with Roy and Mikey, supplied the finishing touches. Usually, however, it was Roy, musically the best educated, who put the melodies into chords and arrangements. Usually George had the lyrics first, and the first song they wrote together with Roy, a number called "'Put It Down,'" pretty much set the pattern for their subsequent efforts. George had the lyrics and the melody for "Put It Down"; everybody then fooled around with it a bit until Jon hit a drum beat, laying down a riff the rest could follow. The other song that survived from these early sessions when the band was groping towards both a songwriting format and a successful musical formula was, "I'm Not Crazy."

George's most controversial contribution to the band, apart from his appearance, is his lyrics. They are quintessentially George. He takes particular pride in his lyrics, in fact. Most people don't understand them, including Boy George himself, whose advice is "to not listen too carefully." He suggests that "if you try to analyze the words too carefully they may seem a bit odd."

The reason for this is that the words come rushing into his head and he copies them down. His lyrics flow in an uninhibited way directly from whatever pops into his mind.

"My music is very egotistical in a sense," he explains, "because I write about myself and my feelings so I can't really think about what it does to other people."

Roy Hay—"Suburban Roy," as George calls him—the insurance clerk/hairdresser who just married his girlfriend, the bride in white, who wants to toy with everything to at least make an effort to understand it, has himself given up making sense of Boy George's lyrics, leaving the question to greater minds than his. "If you sit down," he says, "and pick them apart word by word, you'd probably think 'God, what a *strange* man,' or 'God, what an idiot,' or 'God, what a genius,' but I don't really understand them and I don't even think he does, to be quite honest, because I've seen him write and he doesn't consciously think about what he's writing. He'll just be writing along and he'll come to a word and he'll go, 'What does so and so mean?' and we'll say, 'So and so,' and he'll say, 'Oh, that'll do.'"

"He works so fast that it sort of flows out and that's probably why it sounds so good. He tries to explain the songs sometimes and he makes me laugh because he sits there and someone'll say, 'What does "Church of the Poison Mind" mean?' and I've seen him give about five different replies. I mean, somewhere in there there's probably some sort of reason, but what he does is he writes the lyrics and then looks at them himself and tries to work out a reason."

* * *

While the band kept rehearsing their songs, George was at the same time busy with Sue designing the band's "cultural" look. Sue had somewhere found a book on the secret sign language of tramps and thieves—George was so taken with it he talked about it to everyone. These symbols, printed on colorful outfits, were typical of the mish-mash they worked up. Black-white symbols, gender signs, icons, crosses, Stars of David, Chinese calligraphy, Hebrew script and so on, were profusely put into the signs. It was supposed to mean that Culture Club was open to everyone. It was "contradiction and confusion," two of Boy George's favorite words.

The clothes were individually designed for each member. For George, everything had to be extra large. He couldn't have short sleeves, according to Sue, "because he's got short, fat, hairy arms"; dresses had to be made especially so they wouldn't "make his bum look big"; and the prints, too, had to be "much brighter for him."

Like a Culture Club song—"You can put what you want into it," according to Boy George—the "image" was non-definite. To Jon Moss it was a "good way of presenting symbols without meaning anything specific—just as the band, he said, didn't have "one particular sound."

By the fall of 1981, Culture Club was ready to go on tour. A lot still needed to happen before they would arrive at the smoothed-down sound that was to prove palatable to the "grandfather and baby sister." Creamy synthesizers, back-up singers and musicians, streamlined arrangements and professional producers were still to come into the picture before Culture Club could manufacture a music that would gain acceptance all over the world.

At the time of their first engagements they sounded "really raucous," according to Mikey. But George and Jon wanted to do the "groundwork" on the circuit. George was eager to play the clubs and "get booed at."

Their first date was in Roy's home town, Rayleigh, Essex, at a club called Crocs, a place that catered to a young crowd in their late teens and early twenties. The kids were a typical cross-section of the prevailing youth trend—rockabillies, skinheads, "Kid Creole lookalikes," New Romantics—and their idea of fun was to lay flat out on the floor in a drunken stupor while others danced around them like dervishes. "It was one hell of a place," says Mikey. Some other dates followed, in Birmingham and London, and during Christmas they were back at Crocs.

At these gigs they were still only three instruments—bass, drum and guitar—and George was still having his identity problem with his voice; the tenor did not yet have the "soulful" quality for which it later became known. Mikey was plugging along on the bass, much as he had done when riffing along with the Bob Marley records he'd learned from a sixteen-year-old. Jon Moss kept up the hard-driving beat from the punk bands he'd played with.

The mix was old-fashioned. The essential character, despite the raucousness, was already there: disco-fruity, balmy reggae, a touch of Motown and, occasionally, George crooning with that "soulful ache" he was to eventually master. The sound had the disco, "white boy" funk to it, danceable, with a bumptious teenybopper lilt. The fact that they had been invited back at Crocs gave proof that the kids liked it. Elsewhere, however, there were some "terrible gigs," where the patrons were extremely anti-Culture Club.

The Christmas gig happened to be caught by a record executive by the name of Danny Goodwin. Shortly after New Year's, he walked into The Foundry, where George was mixing up his symbols. Goodwin introduced himself as being with Virgin Records and said "I want a meeting with whoever your manager is. I want your publishing." The upshot was the production of Culture Club's first demo tape, which included "I'm Not Crazy," "Put It Down" and "Kissing To Be Clever."

The tapes were pitiful. Even George was "embarrassed about them." His voice sounded flat. He played the tapes to his parents and some of his relatives and they reacted, "Uh...oh yeah...." Virgin Records felt much the same way; the demos were shelved.

George took it very hard; Jon remained undaunted. By then he had taken full control of the business side of the band, having contacted an old friend, Tony Gordon, from Wedge Records. Not long afterwards, Gordon became their manager; his role was to be crucial in "softening" George's image, recasting it into that of a sexually ambiguous performer, part singer, part clown, capable of gaining wider acceptance. At this point, however, Gordon chiefly helped in pointing out the band's technical shortcomings. He recruited a producer, Steve Levine from CBS, for the next demo recording.

Since Virgin Records had temporarily retreated, Jon decided to utilize George's old connection at EMI, Ashley Goodall. The interest was still there, and they were donated some studio time. "Let's use all these record companies," was Jon's philosophy. "Once one's interested in you they'll all start."

EMI is a major record company. Though it gave Culture Club a studio, the company remained puzzled by the group; George could be a bit much. Once, while the band was recording a song called "The Eyes Of Medusa," the button went down. The recording engineer interrupted, "Excuse me, you're singing about a guy."

"Yeah," George said.

"You're singing about a *man*."

"Yeah."

"You're not allowed to do that."

"I'm allowed to do what I like," George said; the session continued.

Nothing much came of "The Eyes Of Medusa," but the next two tracks they recorded at EMI were to be the making of Culture Club, even though EMI continued to waffle on a full commitment. So they went back to Virgin Records, where Danny Goodwin listened to the demos and signed them up.

The two tracks were "White Boy" and "I'm Afraid Of Me." They were released as singles in May and June of '82.

"I'm Afraid Of Me" bombed, and George, according to Jon, "freaked out."

"White Boy," the first single released, "clicked." George was ecstatic.

A third single, "Do You Really Want To Hurt Me?," released in September of that year, would propel Culture Club into the airwaves around the world, making the name of Boy George a household word on five continents.

It made the Number One slot in twenty-three countries, from Hong Kong to Sweden.

In the U.S. it caused a sensation.

10

Boy George

Just three weeks before the release of "White Boy," twenty-year-old George O'Dowd was complaining about how boring everything about his life was.

The release of "White Boy" changed all that.

It fanned a huge gust of life into his career. Soon the gust was to attain gale force.

It created a new personna.

When the band released "White Boy," everyone was asking "Who's the girl?" and so George adopted the name that was to make him famous.

The song thrust him back into the limelight. He was revived, risen up from boredom. "White Boy" reflected the fears he'd felt before he'd become Boy George, the alienation, the stigma of his early years.

"The whole concept of 'White Boy,'" he explained, is

based on a "kind of empty-headed person." White meant "transparent." White "is someone who's thick, who's like a bottle of milk, someone who is born, gets fat, has lots of kids, and dies, and his sons are like him." Mikey Craig put it more succinctly, "A white boy is any person who's not colorful." In Boy George's second release, the following month, "I'm Afraid Of Me," he appears to be talking about the "white boy" he was once accused of being—the "person who is not colorful." He says, "The song's about this guy I knew, who kept saying, 'You're really white.' I was supposed to be upset by that."

Meanwhile, Virgin Records and Tony Gordon took control of the band. They sent Culture Club on a flying tour of the provinces. Journalists were invited to these appearances, which were spread across England.

The tour was part of Virgin Records' promotional efforts to test the waters for Culture Club's singles and upcoming album. The second phase of putting Boy George across to the kids, concurrent with the June release of "I'm Afraid Of Me," they did universities and clubs in provincial towns. By this strategy, Boy George, the "poser," the "face-about-town," the "Blitz kid," was to win legitimacy as a pop singer.

"You find that if you're in the Midlands kids don't care so much about what you look like," Boy George noted. "The kids who've come to see us have mostly been there because they heard the records and liked the music; they either didn't know what I looked like or else they really didn't care. See, they live in little villages or on farms and they probably only get to hear the records on the radio; and then the only chance they get to buy them is when their parents take them to the shopping centre."

To be accepted in the provinces was a token of musical merit; in the capital, where he'd long been a "curiosity," it would have been harder for him to be taken seriously as a singer of pop tunes.

"In London," he said, "it's really easy to sell records on the strength of publicity, but outside it's not like that at all; a lot of people in town think that if they're on the cover of *Event* or *Record Mirror* they're gonna be Number One. But that's such a load. It's something that I'm beginning to realize more and more."

Virgin Records meant business, so they had to go out, get auditoriums—and inevitably catch some flak. Boy George knew all about that. "When BowWowWow played St. Albans," he remembered, "I heard a skinhead say to his mate, 'Oh, that queer guy's going to come on for the encore, he looks a real state.'" On this tour he'd have to pay his dues with the same hard currency. "Listen," he says, "we didn't get a record deal just by sending photographs to Virgin. We actually did gigs."

On this tour, their rhythmic guitar and percussion had been beefed up with trumpet and sax by producer Levine. They generally opened with a number called "I'm The Boy," swung into "I'm Afraid Of Me," their new single—neither of which made much of an impression—but then got off the ground with "I'll Tumble 4 Ya." There were the tribal rhythms, brassy blasts and reggae riffs—a style, as one reviewer noted, "that would send purists reeling but which, like everything else, had a certain kitsch appeal." Boy George generally loosened up with "Do You Really Want To Hurt Me?," proving, said the reviewer, "that he could stir the emotions with a relaxed, soulful sound."

Reviewer reaction throughout the tour was pretty much favorable. The comments followed a pattern. First: "Boy

George is an arresting sight." Later, the admission: "Culture Club is far less insubstantial than I had feared." At Sherry's in Brighton, the reporter found "each number eminently danceable" and that "Georgie boy soon proved that he is not just a pretty face." At Sherry's they closed with an "exuberant and riotous rendition of 'White Boys' to loud applause."

At Brighton, Boy George wore the outfit that with modifications here and there would remain standard for much of his future appearances all over the world. He was wearing the heavy makeup, the tilted trilby over trailing dreadlocks and a sort of glorified white night shirt. For these early shows he sported dark granny glasses. He had consciously adopted them after the example of John Lennon. At some shows he paid "artistic tribute" to John Lennon, so as to make sure people got the message.

The tour was to end up at the Heaven, a club beneath the arches of Charing Cross. It was to be a bash put on by Virgin Records to celebrate its signing of Culture Club. The company was pleased. The reviews had been good. The *New Music Express*, the most respected trade sheet, gave the band a sort of Seal of Good Musicianship. It liked "White Boy"; it complimented the singer, surprised to hear Boy George sound so "lyrical."

Reviewers also noted the characteristic Culture Club sound, about which other critics were to remark again and again, as the sound rolled over the world, that it was "unclassifiable." As one of the early British critics had it, he was unable to tell whether Culture Club was "ABC, Spandau Ballet, Grace Jones or the Jacksons"—the same confusion that would prevail in America, where people couldn't tell whether Boy George sounded like Smokey Robinson or Janis Joplin. But concerning two elements of this sound, the consensus was already established even back then, when the band was doing the provinces: Boy George had a mellow, soulful voice, and as the Brighton reviewer put it, "His birdlike profile is not particularly appealing, but he does have an endearing line of patter."

As a shakedown, the tour proved helpful in pointing out to the promo-men at Virgin's London offices in Vernon Yard what kinks needed to be worked out of the "image." In the interviews they arranged, Boy George, the notorious "gender bender," the famous "poser" who'd gone around dressed weirdly, hung out with Steve Strange of Billy's, and Jeremiah Healey, and had once lived in abandoned buildings, been identified with the Blitz and modelled for the Uglies. The euphemisms "flamboyant" and "outrageous" now came into use to mean "eccentricity"—a matter of personal taste.

"I've stopped wearing as much makeup lately," Boy George would pointedly inform one reviewer. "I'm cutting down. It's my natural look." They kept asking him questions like, "What's your favorite sexual position, George?" and George, who had learned how to keep the Sunday London tabloids buzzing with his name, could not pass up an opportunity to keep them guessing, "Cuddling," he said, "with all my clothes on."

"Come on, George."

"Embracing, that's my favorite sexual position. What's yours?"

"I'm turning the spotlight on you, George."

"Well, come on then. Ask some questions."

"How honest are you going to be in this interview?"

"I don't know. I might say something different in two days' time."

The exchange would be repeated thousands of times in the following months.

Boy George complained about being tagged a "transvestite." "Everybody thinks I am, but I am not. . . . I am a man! I'm quite manly, actually. I don't think I'm as puffy as I'm made out to be. I'm not gay or anything like that." He was at pains to point out that his songs were like Culture Club, open to everyone. The subject was love, which applied to everyone. "It doesn't just apply to a few people in the room with pink eyebrows and stilettos on." He was "into relationships rather than sexual encounters." He said he wasn't "a scandalous person. I would never ever tell my sex life to the papers."

He was also known for his cutting statements. This reputation had followed him from his days in the abandoned buildings through his time on the androgyny circuit, and he explained how it was: "The best thing to do, if somebody's rude to you, is to look at them and find out their faults, because people have got problems, and if they're going to be rude to you, say, 'God, if I had teeth like yours I wouldn't open my mouth,' or say 'Blimey, at least I'm not eating my way through society,' things like that. Or go up to someone and say, 'I love you in that dress, I never get tired of seeing you in it!'"

His sexuality, for everybody concerned, was clearly a double-edged sword; as a male pop-star wearing lipstick and dresses, he'd be sure to stay in the news, but it might also stand in the way of universal acceptance. In Culture Club's early days, he was already getting quite a bit of hate mail.

The question was never satisfactorily resolved. The idea was to contradict and confuse. It almost seemed as if he were still debating the choice of his own gender. He denied being a "poof," claiming he was "effeminate" in the way he looked, but not an "effeminate" person.

And in the end it didn't matter. The issue was finally skirted not by ingenious denials or repeated explanations.

At last his sexuality was laid to rest in a mist of confusion in which Boy George assumed the "non-specific," unparticular, neutral image the band was trying to project. By the time Culture Club got back to London for their "coming-out party" at the Heaven, one of London's rock music critics was already saying: "After smirking and lurking on the inside and outside of this, that and the other for the past few years—making a name for himself if only because the face didn't suit the name—George has ended up in a position where he will be smart, smack at the centre of a lot of attention. He's going to be a pop star."

The critic spoke for many in the music world when he wrote that Boy George had reached a "new legitimacy."

Before Culture Club got to the Heaven, where the group made its "official" London debut, Boy George had a run-in with the very group that gave their music its special flavor, the reggae-playing Rastafarians, the Jamaican cult that worshipped Ethiopia's former Emperor Haile Selassie. Dreadlocks were part of their religion, and seeing them planted on the singing, strangely dressed boy from Culture Club, the Rastafarians felt that their faith was being mocked. They jeered and hurled catcalls at some of Boy George's appearances, and notice was given that he risked getting beat up. Culture Club had already taken the Rastafarian music and jelled it into their musical mixture.

The "Dreads," as the Rastafarians were called, weren't amused; and Boy George learned that to some people, "symbols" were something more than a haphazard assortment of things used to make one's dress more interesting looking.

"But I'm not doing it to be rude," he said. "I'm just doing it because I like it."

The Rastafarians threatened in vain. They couldn't stop

the combined power of London's music and fashion tribes. While he was still on the road plugging "White Boy," Boy George, along with his old abandoned building friend, Jeremiah Healey, were being hailed as setting the trend for the "white rasta" look. Boy George was singled out as chief among the "Dread End Kids," not only sprouting the snakey strands from his head but also selling "white rasta" designs at his boutique.

Another symbol was also reconsidered. "We've dropped the Star of David now because I've no intention of hurting people's feelings," Boy George explained. "I'm not anti-Arab and I'm not anti-Jew, but I don't like the idea of provoking people, sticking things down their throat."

Nobody, however, came forward to protest against the signs of the tramps and thieves' language, and that symbolism, of which Boy George was particularly enamored, remained the happy possession of Culture Club.

On July 10, 1982, Heaven was packed with over two hundred representatives of London trendiness. If there was a common denominator among the sights and sounds offered by this cavern beneath the Charing Cross arches, it was confusion. But they had come to hear a white band play music that was stepped-down reggae and soul.

Virgin Records and Culture Club had signed a five-year contract. Even now the group was laying down the tracks for the album "Kissing To Be Clever" that would turn out to sell so astoundingly well. However, that success was three months away; as yet Boy George and Culture Club were still no more than the capital's latest flavor of the week.

The fashion accent between the club's various bars and video-viewing spots was on the head. Everybody seemed to be wearing a hat—stove-pipes, rasta woolies, trilbies, big brims. Among the hairstyles, dreadlocks were numerous, as well as plenty of plaits, ponytails and even some beehives.

Boy George's two mentors, Malcolm McLaren and Sue Clowes, were there. McLaren had given George O'Dowd his first big chance, though it hadn't panned out, except to supply Boy George with what one reporter called, "gallons of seedy, sordid BowWowWow gossip . . . yap, snap, titter, snort." Sue Clowes had come to admire the band's duds, into which she'd put months of campy street smarts.

Culture Club's supporting act, Musical Youth, a very young reggae band, came on first and stole the show. The youngsters, almost tots, played with enthusiasm. They had an infectious, innocent grace. They didn't go off the stage until it was almost one o'clock.

Then Boy George came on, clearly at home in the cavern, turning loose with "John Wayne Is Big Leggy!" and bouncing around with dreadlocks flying.

"Culture Club," *Melody Maker* wrote of this debut concert, "creates a glossy sound that attracts without startling you into the revelry of something new. . . . What Culture Club does have . . . is Boy George's fine full, soaring voice. . . ."

11

Do You Really
Want to Hurt Me?

Just a little over three months after the Heaven appearance, Culture Club hit the road on their second British tour. This time the schedule was rather more grueling than it had been previously—a different stop almost every night. The sheet looked impressive, including an early date for a concert in London at Camden Palace, a big hall, to be broadcast by Capitol Radio. Even more impressive was their final stop on November 2 at London's Lyceum, another big house that booked solid bands.

Culture Club seemed to have broken the ice. And as the tour progressed it became clear that it was more than that. They'd made a breakthrough. They'd suddenly crashed into the big-time.

It had begun months earlier when Boy George, as Roy Hay recalls, came up with some lyrics and a semi-melody to go along with them. "We said, 'Yeah, George, let's do it as a lover's rock, a light reggae thing.'

"We got this rhythm box," Hay says, "and started to play around with different tempos and chords. The melody was originally just a G-major progression right through, but you have to embellish what he gives you. We made an arrangement, so it goes up to the C and then to the A-minor. Once we got the melody down, Mikey put down his crucial bass line, and I added guitar afterwards. We all argued a lot and then blended it together."

They played the tune during their early summer tour just prior to Heaven. Meanwhile, Steve Levine, the long-time CBS studio engineer, had introduced the band to a lot of modern technology, such as the Linn Drum and the Fairlight. Levine helped tighten up the production and the arrangements. To fill out the sound, other musicians were brought in: Nick Payne, who played the saxophone, flute and harmonica; Phil Pickett, a keyboard player formerly with a group called Sailor; and a singer with a marvelous and powerful voice, Helen Terry.

One day they did a "take" at the Red Bus Studios. It jelled at once. Nothing further needed be done. Levine and Moss then did the mixing. And that was it.

The song's name was "Do You Really Want To Hurt Me?"

The song that propelled Culture Club to international fame was their third single. It hit the British airwaves in the first week of October, and by the time the band launched its second tour, "Do You Really Want To Hurt Me?" was sitting pretty at Number Two on the charts. By the time the tour ended at the Lyceum, the single had zoomed to the top spot in the British singles chart. At Radio 2, the BBC's national easy-listening station, it was named Record of the Week. A month later, the song hit the top in one country after another. Eventually, the single was to sell more than 6.5 million copies.

With the success of the single, Boy George became an overnight wonder. But not yet a "superstar." That happened shortly afterwards. Just a month after the release of the single, Culture Club came out with their first album, "Kissing To Be Clever."

The album proved that the one hit song had not merely been a flash-in-the-pan. "Kissing To Be Clever" would sell over three million copies, making the band the first since the Beatles to rack up three singles from its debut—"I'll Tumble 4 Ya" and "Time," along with "Do You Really Want To Hurt Me?"

The album was a masterpiece of technical perfection. It was a typical British musical product. Without a native modern rock tradition of its own, England is a laboratory for new sounds. Most of its songsters, guitar heroes, and keyboard wonders are like young lab workers, picking the established, largely American, tunes apart, subjecting them to a sort of spectrum analysis, and then recombining the constituents into a new product. This approach gives rise to the experimentation that creates much of the new British music, from punk to new wave. With the new technology, the studio and engineering skills, the professional arrangers and producers, a good commercial product can be turned out, packaged and marketed with great efficiency. Lately, this process has been picking up, and with groups like Duran Duran, it has taken on a new state-of-the-art efficiency.

"Kissing To Be Clever" was a good example of the British musical scene. Critics quickly fit it into the "genre of slick Euro-dance rock." It was described as a "garish record, a tropical salad of rhythm and gimmicks, bull-fighter horns and dub master raps." The big hit, "Do You Really Want To Hurt Me?," was compared to "weak, watered down fourth division reggae," which starts off with over-blown Motown." But on the whole, the critics were mild. All remarked on the ethnic mix, typically commenting on it as "an infectious synthesizer-bolstered blend of reggae syncopation, Motown-style soul and Latin rhythm and melodies." Culture Club had found the formula for writing "happy little hit records," eminently danceable, with sweetly polished crooning vocals.

Musically, the album was more remarkable for what had been taken out than for what was left in: the hard-driving power of American rock, the rawness of soul, the primitive tropical reggae beat had been removed; the Latin rhythms had been homogenized to the consistency of Tijuana Brass; and having waffed across the Atlantic, the sounds of the Americas—Motown, soul, rock, salsa, calypso, reggae—were turned into sweet, chewy English bubblegum. The Culture Club songs were meant for the audience that made British pop stars famous—fourteen- and fifteen-year-old schoolgirls.

When the album became a smash hit, a guessing game developed among critics as to who Boy George sounded like, as well as to the sources of the different songs. In the blockbusting "Do You Really Want To Hurt Me?," for instance, the weepy guitars were said to be borrowed from the Stylistics' "You Are Everything," and Boy George's misty vocals were said to be inspired by Smokey Robinson's "Ooh Baby Baby."

Boy George has never denied that Culture Club does wholesale "borrowing." The song "Time," for instance, their other big hit of that period, "is sort of Gladys Knight and the Pips." He frankly defends the practice. "Our music is very much rooted in nostalgia. All the best songs that you hear, you listen to them and you say 'that sounds like such and such.'"

According to Boy George, Culture Club is not doing anything other musicians don't do. The difference between their group and the others is that they admit it. He says: "A lot of musicians deny having any musical influences. They're really fooling themselves. I don't think it's anything that happens on purpose—but I think you can't help but pick up on what you hear and what you like.

"Music's really diversifying now. It's becoming apparent that nothing's really original... whether it be fashion or music."

As a singer he was being compared to Jimi Hendrix, Kenny Loggins and Michael Jackson. But almost everyone agreed that his voice was really a carbon copy of Smokey Robinson's (In America, it was said that "Do You Really Want To Hurt Me?" was the best song Smokey Robinson *never* recorded.) Boy George claims, however, that he's always modeled himself on Stevie Wonder. "What white people do when they sing is go for a straight note, but Stevie Wonder and other black singers will change notes, change notes within notes and twist voices."

He's not yet been able to achieve that Stevie Wonder effect, and he's been taking breathing lessons to help him with his singing and to get rid of his asthma, a problem he's had since birth. Though smooth, his voice has a narrow range, and to fill it out, Helen Terry, the group's "gospel-esque" backing singer, was called in. Hers is the voice on "Do You Really Want To Hurt Me?" that gives the richness and depth to Boy George's crooning where it tends to become thin. Helen Terry proved so invaluable that she nearly became a permanent member of the band.

"Helen was really my first opportunity to take somebody

and let them use Culture Club as an elevation for themselves," says Boy George. "Helen is an amazing singer. In comparison, I am just a vocalist; Helen is a great singer. She had never really had a chance before, and when I met her our voices jelled together. She was brilliant at what she did. She fitted in with the album like an instrument."

Helen Terry's was the kind of voice Boy George had been looking for. She was a pro who had been doing session work since she'd arrived in London from Liverpool at sixteen. She'd worked with all kinds of stars, singing backing vocals, for instance, on the famous Lou Reed song "Walk On The Wild Side." For years she'd been singing around London, including in one cabaret that did a spoof version of the Sex Pistols' notorious "Anarchy In The U.D." Boy George caught her act and asked her to sing the backing vocals on "Do You Really Want To Hurt Me?"

In the band's cultural mix, Helen describes herself as the "Bolshevik," the "one that is causing all the trouble. George has this big woman complex; he's really into the big mother figure. Not that he sees me as a mother figure, he just likes the idea."

"The whole idea of calling the album "Kissing To Be Clever," Boy George explains, "is like the kiss of death, the kiss of life. The whole of that album is like a cynical love song."

Boy George describes his songwriting style as trying to "add a different dimension." The cover of the album was to reinforce this idea. "I really like symbols," he says, "so I decided to use the sex symbols on the cover. The picture was really androgynous. It's a heterosexual symbol, but it really doesn't have to be."

He was angry with reviewers who read in "Do You Really

Want To Hurt Me?" all sorts of sado-masochistic implications. "The song is not meant to be provocative," he said. "It could just as well be 'Puppy Love.' The song is about killing someone spiritually with words."

With a Culture Club song, Boy George explained, "You can put what you want into it." He said, "I never write about boys and girls *or* men and men, or whatever." The mellow sound of the music, the crooning voice, the pleasantly pumping tunes meant love and romance. "I want to bring back romance," said Boy George, "and that's what my songs are all about. . . . Everyone I know is so sick of all that punk violence and pessimism. Anyway, the truth is that it's much harder to write a pop song that everyone can relate to than some anthem of hate for a few punks."

When Culture Club got on stage at London's Lyceum for the final gig of the "Kissing To Be Clever" tour, everybody had agreed that the band had rediscovered romance. For twenty years, parents had suffered through a musical generation gap. In the sixties, acid-rock blared out its political/lifestyle message. Then punk brought violence and sex. Now Boy George and Culture Club brought back a sound parents could listen and dance to along with their kids.

When he bounced onto the stage at the Lyceum, he looked happy. His dress and his makeup no longer mattered. He had become "cuddly" and "loveable," and people just wanted to hear him sing. Boy George had come out of the shadowy night life into the brightly lit world of entertainment. The child of the Blitz was now a pop star.

The Lyceum that night was hot and packed with screaming teenage girls. It almost looked like Beatlemania. A lot of the screaming girls were dressed like him; some of the boys were too. They'd copied his hats, his dreadlocks, the billowy clothes, the same bow-lipped Joan Crawford makeup.

The band created a party atmosphere. The girls wanted to touch Boy George. They reached out to touch him and Boy George smiled at them and tried to hold all of their hands. In a few brief months he had managed the impossible—sex appeal without gender.

Sweet, shy and romantic, he crooned and the teenyboppers sighed. The music was clear and sheer and sunny. Boy George was warm. He was wearing his customary Clowes clobber and he had boxing gloves around his neck.

The following night was the same. Two sell-out nights at the Lyceum proved that Culture Club had made it. At the end of each show, colored balloons drifted to the ceiling and couples danced cheek-to-cheek as Boy George crooned, breathily, "Do You Really Want To Hurt Me?"

Still it was hard on him after the show. It would take a while before he could settle into being Boy George, the performer, and he was heard to observe, about the Lyceum shows: "I think that was the loneliest I ever felt. Suddenly people are being nice to me, but it's not to *me*, not really. I don't think I'm someone special, and I'm *not* doing it for that reason, to get people to like me. I don't need people coming up to me and saying, '*Now* you're OK, *now* you're acceptable. I don't want to have anything to do with those people, *ever*. And I don't want them involved with my life."

Boy George

On stage

From the heart

At the airport with Miko

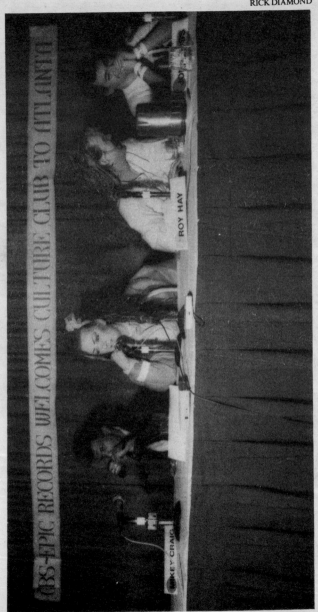

Mickey Craig, Boy George, Roy Hay, Jon Moss

Long live rock!

His dad, Jerry O'Dowd, taught him to fight

With his older brother, Richard

England's fashion sensation

In the spotlight

At WBCN (Boston) with (left to right)
Jon Moss, Mark Parenteau, Tony Berardini

With Oedipus of WBCN

With Debbie Asquith

With Jon Moss

Ready to go

With Jon Moss: playful

With Don Miller, Epic Atlanta PR man

At the airport

The fashion chameleon

12
Top
of the Pops

It was the biggest night in the life of Boy George. "Top of the Pops" was England's top showcase for new talent. For a pop star to get on the show meant that he had reached the big time, that his records would sell and that he had a shot at becoming a superstar.

Just a few weeks before, Boy George could hardly have dreamed of being there. As a kid, he'd sent letters to the BBC asking to be on their pop programs. Now a limo was carrying him to the front door of the studio, where the doorman respectfully opened the door.

Under the bright studio lights, he heard the "Top of the Pops" host, John Peel, introduce him. Boy George worried about his makeup. He touched the ribbons on his hair, arranged the dreadlocks, patted his hat.

Behind him Jon Moss was sitting behind his drums; Roy

Hay fingered the guitar. Mikey stood tensely by his bass. Boy George was always nervous before a show. Jon Moss was an old pro; he didn't bat an eye. The dance floor was filled with boys in fashionable gear and girls wearing miniskirts and flashy dresses.

Millions of homes in Great Britain on that November night were tuned in to the sensational singer who looked like a girl and sounded like a fella. At the O'Dowd home at Shooters Hill, the family sat glued to the screen, waiting for John Peel to finish is introduction.

Boy George's mother was smoking one cigarette after another. Then her son's face appeared in closeup. She had long since stopped bothering about what people thought about George. She thought he looked better, with all his makeup and ribbons, than any girl.

And then she heard the tune that the whole country had been listening to for the past three weeks. "Do you really want to hurt me?" Boy George sang. "Do you really want to make me cry?"

When the set was finished, the band members went down and Boy George followed them. Outside the studio, a young girl named Alison Reed was waiting. She thrust a bunch of red roses into his hands, and Boy George could almost have cried from happiness. He was getting used to being an idol.

The impact of Boy George following the show was like a seismic shock.

"British mums and dads are having fits because the bizarre lead singer of a chart-topping rock group is a Boy," screamed the *Weekly World News* on November 30, in a story titled "Is It A Her? A Him?—Or Is It Neither?"

"Boy George, as he likes to be called," the story went on, "sickens adults by parading around like a floozie, his

96

face painted with makeup and his shoulder-length black hair braided like a Bo Derek."

One parent was quoted, "It wouldn't be so bad, but my sixteen-year-old son finds him attractive. And America is next for this kind of punk rock sickness. It's spreading into other parts of Europe already."

Said an upset mother, "He's not just a bad example—he's disgusting. That thing's got all our children walking around wondering just which sex they are."

Boy George was described as liking to lounge around in a silk kimono and with ribbons in his plaited hair. He said that he didn't think it was something to deny or be embarrassed over.

As "Do You Really Want To Hurt Me?" vaulted to the top of the charts, everybody agreed that it was Boy George's rich tuneful voice and not his freaky appearance that had made him a success. As to his sex life, the burning topic that would never altogether go away, even as Culture Club piled up hit after hit, he patiently elaborated, as he would continue to elaborate in the months to come:

"I get fans of both sexes. Actually, I get more girls after me than the other guys in the band put together. But at present I am not interested in sex at all.

"I'm working so hard at my career that I'm too exhausted by the time I fall into bed for any of that. I lost my virginity when I was sixteen, but sex has never been an obsession with me. It's just like eating a bag of crisps. Quite nice but nothing marvelous. Sex isn't exactly black and white, there's a lot of gray."

And he added, "You can think what you want of me. I'm not bothered."

While England went into a tizzy, George's parents took it all in stride. His nineteen-year-old brother, Gerald, an amateur boxer who worked on a building site, admitted that his mates often teased him about George's bizarre looks.

Boy George's mother also admitted that her son's new fame had brought a lot of unwanted attention. She said, "People do nudge each other and make awful comments when they see him. 'Doesn't he look like a girl? they would say to me."

"My answer is always, 'Yes, I'll bet a lot of girls would like to look as good as George does.' But I don't think he's homosexual."

She told the interviewer, "He's always been such a loving son. He phones me every day and visits us every weekend. When his dad had a heart attack, he was so busy I didn't tell him until his dad was out of intensive care. He cried, 'You should not have done that, Mum!'"

During the interview at his parents' home, Boy George was sitting next to his brother Gerald, who is well-muscled and clean-cut. Boy George was wearing white dracula makeup and blood-red lipstick. He said he got on very well with his parents.

"They know that beneath all this makeup and the clothes I am pretty normal. Well, I think I am."

Reaction to Boy George's appearance on the television show was not only registered by outraged parents or the intense clamor of fans, both of which grew overnight from a groundswell into a massive wave. Nothing like Culture Club and Boy George had been seen before in Britain since the Beatles; Britain's top show biz personalities chimed in with a sober appraisal of the singer's talents.

They welcomed the new star in their midst. All the top entertainment figures were agreed that behind the bizarre character there was the true talent to stay the course.

Petula Clark remarked: "'Do You Really Want To Hurt Me?' is the kind of record that could have been a hit years ago. His is a curious mixture of unusual looks and very straightforward records, which is clever. I like what he does and if he wrote me a song I would certainly record it."

Boy George also received praise from Britain's top disc-jockey, Mike Read. "He has a superb voice in the old-fashioned sense."

Rod Stewart simply said, "He's got the most soulful voice I have heard in years."

George Martin, the Beatles' record producer, observed, "Boy George is one of the more memorable people of the new breed of talent. He has a much better voice than half the others around, and definitely has a future."

Tom Jones said he was a Boy George fan. "I've heard Boy George and like his records."

All the figures from Britain's show biz world agreed that apart from the lasting quality in his voice, Boy George was also humorous, witty and interesting.

The next release to hit the British charts and to keep Culture Club in the limelight was the single "Time." This song was written with a different approach. It came from Roy and Mikey getting some music together and George becoming excited and putting the words to it.

At first, it didn't come out very well, bland and unspirited. Then Mikey fooled around a little and came up with a staggered beat that sounded good. Roy said, "Let's do it with the Moog." And so they produced the great snare sound and the whole thing came together.

The song became their third big hit in a row, and it finally broke the ice in the U. S. They'd already been negotiating a deal with CBS for some time. But the American record executives weren't sure that someone looking like Boy George would be acceptable to the American public. CBS had been hesitant about the material until they heard "Do You Really Want To Hurt Me?" Then they heard "Time," and that gave them more confidence.

After scoring its big hit in England, "Time" quickly moved in the U. S. into the Top Five on the pop singles chart. The deal with Epic, the CBS label, was made, and in order to see what the American reaction would be to a boy with dreadlocks, plucked eyebrows, heavy makeup and flowing robes, Culture Club in late '82 flew over to New York for a brief two-day stint at the Ritz, a real musical "in" place of rock and reggae, where the group had their first live American exposure. Three more American tours, much more extended than this brief stand, would follow, and upon each return Boy George would show himself in better form.

With one hit in the U. S., and with "Time" shaping up to be another one, Boy George realized that he couldn't rest easy until he'd proved that Culture Club had really broken in by establishing itself as a permanent name like the Beatles.

"It's great having a hit," he said. "A lot of English bands come over on the storm, Human League and Soft Cell, and bands like that and they have hits, but you just have to keep that momentum going. I think it's all very nice— people flashing cameras and people getting crazy—but I think the most important thing is the music, and what it boils down to, at the end of the day, is that if you haven't got the music, you better give up."

Boy George's androgynous figure and "cuddliness" was to make him a "curio" in the U. S., but virtually from the moment he'd finished his set on "Top of the Pops" in the Fall of '82, he became England's number one topic. He has remained a national obsession to this day. If anything, the obsession has continued to grow. He and Princess Diana fill the papers almost daily.

Boy George has had to learn to deal with it, just like any other famous person. "I'd been trying to be a star for so long," he says, "it's nice to finally be one. In a lot of ways, I'm like Princess Diana; I've had to cope with everything from scratch."

He'd come a long way from the time when as a young lad he used to stand at the bus stop, clowning around to spark a laugh in the people waiting in line. Now he was amusing people all over the world. He was proud of his achievement. "It is good for a person with working class origins like me to have made something out of nothing."

But he soon learned that being the second most famous face in England had its drawbacks. On the street, people were always yelling out of car windows, "Hey George, why don't you stop wearing all that makeup."

One result of being famous was being constantly called upon to defend his tastes. He tried to make people understand that his makeup was a part of himself, that he'd been applying it from the time he'd entered his teens. He was proud that he could do his makeup really well, better than most women. He would be really upset if his makeup came out badly.

Not only were his makeup and clothes the subjects of never-ending fascination to the British press; everything about him was. Boy George was no longer a "weirdo" who hung around the clubs, an outrageous "poser" and "bad boy." He'd become a "famous weirdo" with a giant following of fans who tried to dress like him and laid siege to his door. Suddenly all sorts of people from his past were being sought out by enterprising reporters, and the pages of the tabloids bloomed with their often spiteful reminiscences.

Boy George would never get used to the journalistic pot shots and low blows, and from the moment he walked off the set of "Top of the Pops" in November '82, he had a hard time of it in the British dailies and weeklies.

People out of his past, whom he hadn't heard from in years, were suddenly all over the papers with revelations about him. Given the sensationalistic tone of England's tabloid press, these revelations were invariably nasty and backbiting.

One of his friends from his early teens, Beryl Richards, told of the beginnings of Boy George. Beryl and George O'Dowd used to go together to the Black Prince disco in Bexleyheath every Thursday night.

"George used to sing even then," Beryl recalled. "We used to go into London, clubbing, and he would sing on the train on the way home—pop songs or whatever we'd heard in the clubs." Beryl said that George at that time "had shortish hair and punky-ish clothes. . . . I don't remember him getting into much trouble."

The reporters sought out the people who had known George during the years he was living in abandoned buildings. One of these, Stephen Jones, a trendy hatmaker, recalled a fight he had witnessed between George and Jeremiah Healey. "They always had this love-hate relationship," Jones told the reporter. "I came out of my workshop one day and they were screaming up and downstairs, in and out of rooms.

"His sharp tongue is usually reserved for people who deserve it. . . . He gets wild but he can be very humorous, too."

Another young man, an ex-friend, who said he'd been very close to George, nastily remarked that beneath the bizarre clothes and makeup there was a "rather grubby bloke."

Gleefully, the tabloids served up every spiteful bit of

news they could find about Boy George. According to the tabloids, George seemed to always have explosive relationships with his friends. Philip Salon and George "used to scream at each other for hours," it was reported. "George was always telling Philip how ugly he was." Salon himself related to the paper how he and George often had to make a run for it. "People were always taking a violent exception to the way we looked. Then they'd try to beat us up."

Another old friend of George's, Michael Eggleton, who'd first met George around the clubs and palled around with him when both were about sixteen, volunteered to talk to one tabloid, reminiscing at length about the time they'd spent together hanging around the rock clubs, trying on clothes and running away from Teds.

"We got most of our jewelry and clothes from junk shops and Oxfam and we would give the junk shop people a laugh by trying on the old hats and dresses. One night every week a club called Billy's in Soho was taken over by trendies like us. It became known as 'Bowie Night.'"

Eggleton said, "George loved having his picture taken—often in picture booths—and was always ready to shock. We liked to go to Oxford Street on Saturdays and George would stand out among the crowds with his spiky hair and weird clothes."

While Boy George's celebrity status continued to grow, the nasty stories in the garish press grew likewise. Seeking out people who had known him in the two clubs, Billy's and the Blitz, where George had spent much of his youthful years, reporters found girls who readily contributed their bit to the almost daily attacks on the new pop star. It seemed as if the papers were only intent on character assassination.

One girl told a reporter that she had known George at the Blitz and that once when she "tried to have a look at the hat he was wearing" he'd told her, "If you touch it I'll smash your bloody face in."

A photographer who used to snap George and his friends at the clubs said, "There was a club called Billy's that was the trendiest place in London before the Blitz opened. That's where George's character seemed to change. He'd throw jealous dramas over really trivial things, like if someone nicked his makeup ideas."

Peter Dawson, the headmaster at Boy George's old Eltham Green School in Southeast London was also queried about the famous pop star he had expelled six years previously. He described Boy George in his school days as a "classic example of the word 'misfit.'" He did not fit in and he did not want to. He did not get on with his teachers and he did not get on with the other boys and girls.

"He was a perpetual truant," Dawson recalled. "He would not come to school and would not work when we got him there. . . . If he asked to leave the classroom that would be the last you saw of him."

Boy George's boyhood girlfriend, Tracie Birch, whom he has credited for encouraging him to wear "extreme" clothes, recalled for the newspapers how they'd go to a club and "dress up really outrageously."

Tracie said: "We'd get into all sorts of trouble, but I always used to stick up for him. He'd never stick up for himself." She also told the press that it just didn't occur to him to make advances. I fancied him like mad, but I realized we'd never be more than friends. He wouldn't even hold my hand, let alone give me a kiss. Once I threw my arms around him to give him a hug, and all he said was, 'Mind my makeup.'"

All the attention in the press, however, whether good or bad, was only an indication of the enduring fascination the public had developed for the world's first androgynous pop star. Within a year, his sexuality ceased to be an issue—only his "personality" and music mattered.

An English psychologist explained: "Boy George is not sexually threatening; if he were he wouldn't have been so successful. He appears *asexual*." A sex researcher said, "George has been very brave. Men with feminine streaks are attractive, more understanding, easier to live with. He appears to have no sexual problems. He probably has a low sex drive."

British mums and dads, boys and girls, housewives, grannies, secretaries, truck drivers and even the royal family and the British parliament would at last fall under his spell. He had been accepted by all age groups and become a respectable household name. He was as British as fish and chips. England's housewives voted him "Personality of the Year."

Just a little over a year after Culture Club's conquest of the pop charts all over the world, Boy George would be invited to give a royal command performance (Culture Club had replaced Duran Duran as Princess Di's favorite group) and the House of Commons would put a motion before Parliament congratulating Boy George on Culture Club's recent Grammy award.

The motion said: "This House congratulates Culture Club, the Police, Duran Duran and other British stars on their success in the Grammy awards; and acknowledges the enormous pleasure they bring to millions of people around the world and the exports they and their industry achieve for the United Kingdom."

13

Colour
by Numbers

"You're only as good as your last record," Boy George mused one day. "It's like with Michael Jackson when he brought out 'Off The Wall.' I thought that was it, because it was such a great album. For somebody to follow 'Off The Wall' with 'Thriller,' that's an achievement. Every time you write a record you think that's the last thing you're going to do. On the whole you can't be optimistic, you've just got to play it by ear and instinct. I mean basically we're not particularly trained musicians—the whole of what you do is by instinct, it's amazing."

Culture Club's "instinct" resulted in its second monster album, "Colour By Numbers," with four equally monstrous hits, "Karma Chameleon," "Church Of The Poison Mind," "Miss Me Blind" and "It's A Miracle." The songs were written in the usual fashion. "We spent ten weeks arguing," says Boy George, "and we wrote the album in ten days. We spend weeks throwing cups of coffee over each other and smashing guitars and eventually we write a good album. That's the way it is with music."

As soon as "Kissing To Be Clever" had taken off, the band had felt the pressure to repeat that first success and prove that it wasn't a fluke. The pressure was all the stronger during 1983. George's fears were eased when "Church Of The Poison Mind," released as a single in April of 1983, became a giant smash both in England and the U. S. The album, in fact, received even greater acceptance than did the first one.

On the whole it was softer, "toned down" in the same manner that Boy George became muted as fame overtook him. "The first album was young and raw," says Mikey Craig. "It was full of ideas and energy. Those ideas are better executed on the second album. It might open another audience to us, perhaps an older audience. It's still pop, but it's a lot easier to take in."

There's a decided American feel to the album. "We were in America a lot just before we recorded the second album," explains Mikey, "and obviously George was listening to a lot of ballad-type things—it kinda put him in a smooth mode and the album went likewise. We got into an attitude of wanting to write pop songs. It was very simple—we all decided and agreed upon it."

Craig called the second album "more digestible," and the general consensus seemed to agree with him. The ten songs on the whole were described as being "well-crafted" and pleasing to the ear without threatening to make waves. Black commentators noted that the album was "very black . . . very soulful." The album established Boy George as a "blue-eyed soul balladeer of the first rank."

Boy George himself described the album as "very vocal. People might say it's softer, but actually it's bigger. There's a lot of harmony, a lot more voice work and a lot of sax this time. It's more acoustic than the last one, not as much electronics. It's a more edible version of 'Kissing.'"

Though "softer," "Colour By Numbers" contained the same recognizable blend of musical influences, with the addition of a new country sound ("Karma Chameleon"), along with the usual strains of reggae, gospel, easy listening and Motown. Boy George was again likened to Smokey Robinson (especially in "Mister Man"), this time with an element of the rich gospel fervor of Gladys Knight. There were four support musicians, and Helen Terry again lent her background blues-belting voice to the musical flavor, especially in "Church Of The Poison Mind," in which she engages in a stirring gospel-like exchange with Boy George. "She can nearly sing me into the ground," says Culture Club's lead vocalist.

The other quality of the band's music—its danceability—was also very much evident on the new offering. And the other by-now recognized hallmark of the group's sound, Boy George's mellow voice with its Motown flavor, again received its share of raves. Though clearly trendy British commercial pop, critics credited it with being better than a cut above the other representatives of this "sugar-candy" school, such as Haircut One, ABC or Wham!

All of the ten tunes had the kind of "hook" that made them stick, but none more so than "Karma Chameleon," which hit the British pop charts almost immediately after its release as a single. It had bluesy harmonica licks and Helen Terry, multi-tracked, echoing Boy George's lines.

Boy George says he wrote this song way back at school. "It was a really old tune that I had which Roy wouldn't work out because he hated it so much. It was like 'Kumbaya,' y'know, 'ging gang goolie goolie goolie goolie,' and he wouldn't play it. I just said, 'It's a *great* song, you'll see.'"

He says it embodies two things: his belief in karma and his distrust of people who change their colors. "I believe if you're cruel, you get paid back in little ways," he explains, "little things like kicking your toe in the morning or cutting yourself when you shave.

"As for chameleons, it's nice to have people around you you trust, so they don't keep changing their opinions. Especially in the situation I'm in, it's very difficult for me to have friends. It's difficult to trust people. I find it very depressing sometimes." The words "red, gold and green" that occur in the song are the colors of the Rastafarian flag, which Boy George equates with a special symbolic idealism significant to himself.

"Church Of The Poison Mind" recalled to most people Stevie Wonder's "Uptight," with ecstatic rhythms and a bumptious wailing harmonica. Boy George explains the song as being "based on the Japanese idea that your brain is the temple of your body. It's basically a love song about how people get trapped by their own emotions. I'm saying that every new relationship is a new experience and you should take everything as it comes and not be trapped in 'The Church Of The Poison Mind.'"

The songs reflect a grab bag of cultural smatterings; there's carnival-like, pop-soul calypso in "It's A Miracle"; again, calypso-flavored funk in "Stormkeeper" and "Miss Me Blind"; a bit of Burt Bacharach in "Changing Every Day." For "poppy" tunes lovers are supposed to dance to, the songs generally show a kind of romantic and dismal side of life. In "Mister Man," Boy George blames masculine aggression for the world's woes; in "Stormkeeper" and in "Victims," the subjects are emotional outlaws.

"Black Money" is a mournful metaphor for infidelity showing hauntingly in the gospel-like dialogue between Boy George and Helen Terry, the sinister exchange between two people trading in false emotions.

Of all the songs in "Colour By Numbers," "That's The Way" is most legibly autobiographical, depicting Boy George's painful childhood. "It's about school," he explains. "It's about parents. It's about when you're a child and you've been out on a wonderful day trip and you want to tell your parents about it, and the first thing they say is, 'Shut up, I'm watching TV.' The line 'clowns caress you' is related to teachers. It's basically saying when a child is growing up you should listen to it and help it and not shut it up."

There was one other very personal note to "Colour By Numbers"—the three numbers, five-thirty-eight, in the corner of the album. It was something George came up with himself. The "five" stands for "heart," because there are five letters in the word; the "three" stands for "I love you," because it is made up of three words; and the "eight" stands for the combination of five and three, combining the meaning and emotion of the first two numbers.

14 ||
CCC

The Dominion Theatre stands in the heart of one of London's busiest crossroads. It's seen a lot of action in its days but nothing like the unbelievable melee spilling out onto the pavement at the bottom of Tottenham Court Road on the dusky final day of March, a year ago.

Two ambulances are parked outside the theatre. Fortunately, there will be no casualties, except for one young girl with a headache because of the noise.

The noise is inseparable from the event, because this is a Culture Club concert with Boy George, the biggest pop phenomenon since the Beatles. Without the noise of thousands of screaming girls, a swaying mass crammed in front of the stage squealing and shrieking and reaching out with clawing hands, such an event is inconceivable.

At other appearances girls have fainted. Girls, in excitement, have tumbled off the seats on which they stood up to catch a better glimpse of their heartthrob.

The fans are mad about the Boy. At the Dominion they screech and clamor, pushing up against the glass doors of the lobby—and it's still only seven o'clock: the show has not even begun.

The girls range from their early teens to mid-twenties. They belong to the immense following that has sprung up in the wake of the Boy George landslide. They've got their hair in dreadlocks, some of them stick-on—that is, nylon plaits that cost as much as seventy-five dollars. They've got plucked eyebrows and white faces, painted with mascara, panstick and pearly eye shadow; they're wearing painted straw hats, ribbons, Kung-fu slippers and colorful, squiggle-cluttered Sue Clowes imitation clothes and dark John Lennon glasses. They're called "CCC"—"Culture Club Clones."

In England, the CCC makes up a mammoth contingent wearing Culture Club T-shirts and Culture Club sweatshirts. Their names are prefaced with the gender designation—they're now Girl Janet, Girl Shirley, Girl Lisa.

The CCC love Boy George.

Girl Irene says: "I just want to cuddle him."

Girl Shireen: I've never really thought about meeting George. It's beyond my wildest dreams."

Girl Joanne: "I'd love him to tickle me with his dreadlocks."

Girl Kimberley's dream is to take a drive on a hot summer day in a two-seater sports car with Jon Moss at the wheel and herself seated on Boy George's lap.

Girl Patsy gave up her job so she could follow Culture Club on tour in Europe and America. Girl Andrea follows Culture Club around England in the hope that one day she'll be permitted "to wash and iron their stage gear."

The CCC send Boy George four-foot-high Valentine's cards. They cover their bedroom walls with pictures of Boy George. They travel hundreds of miles just for a glimpse of their idol. For them, a Culture Club concert is a celebration of their love for Boy George.

The show at the Dominion is typical. After the house lights dim, the screaming starts even before Boy George lopes barefoot onto the stage. A hail of objects—trinkets, roses, scraps of paper with telephone numbers, even the occasional bottle of champagne—is thrown at his feet. At some other shows, Boy George will wait out of sight before bouncing into the spotlight, building up the excitement, teasing the crowd by singing in the wings until the hysteria reaches a high point and he dances into view.

He sings sweetly the Culture Club mixture of black and white pop with touches of soul. The band plays well. Occasionally, Helen Terry lets rip with her powerful voice. Boy George delights the audience by cuddling the fluffy toys thrown up on the stage.

He sways his hips and beckons and makes tongue-rolling trills. He is a showman. He is a clown. He is a funnyman crooning about love. When he removes his dark granny glasses, the screaming reaches an overwhelming pitch.

He sings the standard hits, and some new ones like "Church Of The Poison Mind." Between the songs, he dances and throws out chatty lines and patter. The lines will vary from show to show, but they're almost always about makeup. The audience never fails to respond. They love it.

He enjoys playing before kids. "They don't think they're better than you are," he says. He feels happy and secure entertaining them. Perhaps he himself stopped developing emotionally at an early stage—at the stage when he began to feel that nobody loved him. Since then, despite an adolescence spent on the streets and in clubs, he's been a child who loves to paint his face, dress up, show off and clutch cuddly dolls. At his concerts, he's not playing *for* kids but *with* them.

He is *Boy* George, not because he dresses like a girl, but *boy* as *child*, the stage that is neutral, before maturity sets in and the one gender separates into the two sexes.

Towards the end of 1983, the CCC boom had become an epidemic and Boy George a national obsession. The papers were filled with him. And Boy George look-alikes were legion.

The boys had followed the girls and were now dressing and using makeup like Boy George. The CCC phenomenon even spread to young adults, some of them married.

It was a "trendy" fashion, just as the Beatles had spawned long hair for boys in the sixties. Again, it was an example of music influencing fashion. Boy George and Culture Club had created a giant party atmosphere. People participated by going about as guests at a fancy-dress ball. Every day at school, on the street, at the office, at home—all the places that in England are so drab—it was Halloween.

A lot of youngsters started dressing up after first hearing Culture Club. It wasn't the other way around. The music got them into the party atmosphere. As a result, the CCC movement spread like wildfire, as all people—especially kids—like a party!

CCC took the country by storm. By the end of '83, there were so many Boy George "clones" that when a Boy George look-alike mugged a woman in London, the police said they were hampered in their search for the thug because there were so *many* youngsters looking like Boy George. It was especially confusing to American tourists. One "clone" reported he'd been stopped by some. "They wanted to smudge one of my eyebrows," he said (He didn't bother to tell them he wasn't Boy George because "they'd have been too disappointed").

Aimed at the CCC-crowd, articles appeared with makeup tips explaining just how Boy George achieved his effect. Mary Lou, a top makeup artist, analyzed how the famous pop star did it:

"The first thing he has done," she wrote, "is shave off his eyebrows, and draw on this strange oriental shape with black eyebrow pencil." She described how he next applied a heavy white foundation on his face, shaded his jawline, followed the lines of the cheekbones with black shading powder, taking it up into the temples and hairline, and exaggerated the outline of his mouth with black pencil before filling it in with a deep red lipstick.

Mary Lou further explained how Boy George managed to make his nose look longer and narrower by shading it with light brown eye shadow. As to his eyes, she said that Boy George had mastered a technique of eyelining many women may find difficult—putting a black eye pencil line 'round the inside rim and another one outside the lashes, applying black mascara to the lashes and gold-shine eye shadow on his eyelid.

With such tips, the Boy George look-alikes were able to keep up with their idol. Top of the doubles was sixteen-year-old Darren Hogg, who achieved national fame by winning a Boy George look-alike contest. Afterwards, he complained that he had to be constantly dodging Boy George fans, who mistook him for the real McCoy. He looked so much like the original that even his friends began calling him George. Hogg created a sensation in the south of France, where hordes of French autograph-seekers besieged him.

For a while he carried on with the imposture. He recommended that everyone use makeup, "even old men."

The Boy George look-alikes claimed that their dress and makeup made them really popular with the girls. One eighteen-year-old building worker related that when he first dressed up as Boy George, "it was a real eye-opener—the girls were all over me." Wearing makeup, he claimed, "just improves you so much."

Married Boy George look-alikes shop for new cosmetics just as their wives do. They buy lipstick, eye shadow and lots of foundation and rouge. They say that usually their wives or girlfriends encourage them to look like Boy George and that they help them make outfits similar to those worn by the Boy. The wives think their husbands look "sexy" in makeup.

Nevertheless, there is no need to fear a wholesale conversion to the fad. A survey in England revealed that only three women out of a hundred liked the idea of their men wearing lipstick.

Boy George himself believes that his influence is far from tainting the morals of youngsters. "I think," he says, "there are a lot of people in the press who think that we're corrupting young people, but in fact we're making them more intelligent because what we're doing is we're telling them to be themselves.

"We're not telling them to look at us as some kind of demigods, you know, with a phallic symbol like a guitar and tight jeans, we're telling them we're not perfect. We're dealing with much more interesting things than rock and roll and sex. We're dealing with imperfections, we're dealing with things that go on in society, things that affect real people. That's why people like us.

"And, also, one thing I should say, a lot of those young

kids, they're much more intelligent than, you know, you ever imagine they are. There was a little girl on the news in Detroit, thirteen years old, who turned around and said, 'Boy George is not telling men to be women, or women to be men, he's saying do what you feel.'"

Boy George has been pleased about the "clone" cult he has spawned among his fans, but not about the "clones" in the musical field. "The amazing thing is that when I first went 'round the record companies nobody wanted to know me because they said I was too weird. But now they all seem to be desperate to find somebody who looks a bit like me in any way at all. I suppose it's flattering—but sometimes it's a bit annoying."

One such mimic is "Marilyn," whose real name is Peter Robinson, a twenty-year-old boy who looks and dresses like Marilyn Monroe. Peter Robinson has signed a $150,000 contract with a large record company. He has done a successful single, "Calling Your Name," which made Number Three on the charts. Peter did another single, "Cry And Be Free," which was also successful. The papers report that Peter is working on his debut album and that an American cable television company wants to do a series with him.

Boy George and "Marilyn" went back to the days when they shared the abandoned building on Clarburton Street. Peter had been part of the bunch that included Philip Salon, Steven Strange, Haysi Fantayzee and the then George O'Dowd that got up dressed to the nines, making the rounds of clubs and surviving—since none of them worked—by looking outrageous enough so that people took their photos and gave them free food and drinks.

Peter and Boy George had been close in those days. Together they'd landed a job at the Blitz; one night a week,

Tuesday night, George ran the cloakroom while Peter worked as a waiter.

When photographers snapped "Marilyn" and Boy George at Heathrow Airport returning together from a holiday in Egypt, the picture of the two with their heavy makeup and long plaited hair created an immediate sensation. The photograph was flashed around the world. The picture turned Peter Robinson into an instant star. Overnight, "Marilyn" became a celebrity and almost immediately afterwards signed a six-figure contract with Phonogram Records.

Peter Robinson claimed that his association with Boy George had nothing to do with his lucrative recording deal. "I didn't want to be photographed with Boy George, but what do you do?" he shrugged.

"He was annoyed with me afterwards. Everyone told him I was using him to get publicity and when you've got that many people around you telling you something you start to believe it. But a boy dressing up as Marilyn Monroe is a news item in itself, so I really don't need anyone else's help to get publicity."

Relations between them became very strained when Boy George heard the hit record "Calling Your Name," because the song had the same kind of light pop/R&B sound which has come to be associated with Culture Club.

Boy George dismissed it, saying, "When a record company signs somebody like Marilyn, their attitude is that if we can have half of what Culture Club's got, we're fine."

Peter Robinson, like Boy George, came from an unhappy environment and began "dressing up" and wearing makeup out of a need for attention. Born in Jamaica, his parents split up when he was three. He says his school experience had a lot to do with his "transformation."

"In England, you get these people at school who think

they show they are very clever by picking on people who are fat or wear glasses or are slightly pretty or feminine," he recently recalled. "And that happened to me.

"Ever since I was about five, kids used to call me 'poof' or 'queer.' As time went on, they tried to outdo each other. Finally, someone came up with 'Marilyn.' By this time I was in my teens and I thought, 'Fine, you call me Marilyn, you idiots, but let's see who has the last laugh.'"

George and Peter had been friends for nearly five years when their friendship ended in the feud which was mostly conducted through the media. Their rift has made the world's most famous pop star philosophical about friendship. "Eccentric people rarely have true friends," he says today.

"I think it's very difficult because people never really know what they're dealing with. I think you're lucky in your whole life to have more than two or three real friends. Real friendship is when you can call up at three in the morning and say, 'I'm dying, please come over and bring some bandages.'

"The most important thing to me is my family. They're the only people I really care about. And the audience, they're the people who are making us what we are. They're who you care about. They become your friends."

15

America

At the end of Culture Club's spring '84 tour of the U.S., a festive gathering took place in Atlanta. In the large conference room of CBS' Epic Record Division, Don Dempsey, chief of Epic Records, got up to make a speech. As he spoke he was looking past the rows of Epic and CBS Video executives to Boy George, Jon Moss, Mikey Craig and Roy Hay.

Dempsey mentioned, by way of introduction, that Epic is the home of Michael Jackson, who recorded "Beat It." Then he mentioned a number of other artists in its roster. He went on:

"One thing you have to understand is that artists do not come to record companies in a collective way. They come to a company one at a time. So when you look at a big company, a very successful company, you have to understand that the artists that are there are selected for very special and unique reasons." Raising his voice slightly, Dempsey said, "This brings us to Culture Club."

"What did we see in them? Was it fashion? Jump in, make a quick buck, on to the next whatever happens in this business? Well, fashion comes and goes, artistry stays. George and Jon and Roy and Mikey are outstanding songwriters, professional musicians, and while the impact of video had a staggering and positive effect on the music industry it still comes down to songs people relate to.

"This band has been racking up hit after hit. Their music has no color barrier. Their records have enjoyed the same success in the black music charts as they have in the pop and rock music charts.

"In my mind," Dempsey went on, "Culture Club's popularity has a lot to do with the fact they do not talk down or play down to people, and George, as I understand him, is friends with everyone who is friends with him. Their debut album was the first debut album in twenty years to produce three singles in the Top Ten. Amazingly, their follow-up album has accomplished the very same thing.

"The award we are presenting on behalf of Epic/Virgin Records has to do with the fact that this band has sold over five million albums in the U.S.A., and if you add the singles sales that they've also made in America, you have a total of ten million sales of singles and albums by this wonderful band here."

Dempsey paused and applause filled the room. The speaker continued, "So on behalf of all of us at Epic and in the good old U.S., I'd like to present the Culture Club...."

Again applause filled the room. All eyes were on Boy George, Jon, Mikey and Roy as they held up five platinum records.

* * *

Dempsey made it sound as if it had been love at first sight between Epic and Culture Club. It hadn't been quite so smooth as all that. Just as Boy George had to win acceptance in England, he had faced a similar obstacle in the U.S. If anything, American record companies had been more cautious than their British counterparts. At Epic the initial feeling was that even if people went for the Culture Club music, they might get turned off once they saw the image of Boy George with lipstick, dreadlocks and Raggedy-Ann frocks.

Epic's talent scout, Greg Geller, had first heard "White Boy" when it came to him as a single in its original black-and-white sleeve. Though in the photo Boy George was decked out in his customary flamboyant regalia, the black-and-white picture did not convey the impact Boy George would have had in color. Geller didn't really pay attention to what Boy George looked like. He listened to "White Boy," didn't like it very much, and there the matter hung until a few months later he received another Culture Club single, "I'm Afraid Of Me."

This time Geller was impressed. He liked the music. He particularly liked the voice of Boy George. He played the record over and over. He also gave more careful study to the picture on the sleeve.

It was a very striking sleeve. It showed Boy George, this time in color, in full feather, with his hair in braids, wearing a straw hat, a face obviously made up, and in the Hebrew-lettered Sue Clowes clothes. Though he didn't believe "I'm Afraid Of Me" would be a hit, Geller wanted to sign the group, believing they had a future. Then came "Do You Really Want To Hurt Me?" and Epic's talent scout decided that that was the clincher. He told the marketing people that

125

they were going to hear a new band from England.

The sweetly crooning voice of Boy George filled the conference room singing, "Do-you-really-want-to-hurt-me?"

Everyone around the table fell to snapping their fingers. Don Dempsey, Epic's chief, snapped right along. When the tape was over everyone clapped their hands.

A week later, at the next marketing meeting, Geller replayed the tape. Again everyone liked it. This time, in fact, they liked it even more.

The following week Geller was able to inform the marketeers that finally he'd gotten hold of a video. But he warned them, "The singer does not look the way you expect him to look."

At this period the record industry happened to be undergoing a revival. After a decade of flat sales, a whole "new music" movement heralded the comeback of the U.S. record industry.

The "new music" appealed to black and white audiences alike. It was even luring the older generation back into the record shops. When Men At Work pressed their first album, the average age of the buyer was twenty-five; it sold more than four million copies, topping any other 1982 release. When the follow-up album reached the record shops, it sold over one million albums in three weeks. "Now record companies are falling all over each other to sign new musical acts that, a year ago, they wouldn't touch with a ten-foot pole," said one music industry insider.

Frank Dileo, now Michael Jackson's manager, but then promotions vice president for Epic, reflected a new boldness on the part of big record companies hungry for a piece of the newly rejuvenated pop record business. "Stations are crying for new stuff," Dileo said at a time when a debut album was considered promising if it sold over 50,000 copies.

At that time at least a dozen of the "new music" debut albums had passed the 500,000 mark, and five had topped a million. Twenty-three of Billboard's top one hundred best-selling albums had come from "new musicians," most of whom were part of what has been called the "second British invasion" in American rock music. After hearing Boy George sing what would become a mammoth world-wide hit, Epic's executives, recognizing a fresh new sound, were willing to gamble on Boy George's outrageous appearance.

It was a gamble. Even Boy George acknowledged that. He was aware that people in England were used to seeing bands that looked a little different. On the eve of his U.S. tour, he had the jitters. "I don't know how people are going to react to Culture Club there," he said.

He realized that America was the testing ground. "In America it's like we're a new band. People don't know about us. So if you don't get off on the music you don't get anywhere."

No pop star in England can claim true stature until he's conquered America. The British groups that rank high to-day, from the Beatles to the Police, hold that position by virtue of the fact that Americans by the millions buy their records, go to their concerts and listen to them on the radio. The five platinum records George, Jon, Mikey and Roy received in Atlanta proved to Boy George that Culture Club was now an established fact.

Dreadlocks and lipstick and earrings had nothing to do with his success in America. In fact, many who first heard his soulful crooning voice on the radio believed he was black. Even some black radio stations were initially fooled. So America has paid Boy George the tribute of taking him on his merits alone. Here there was no history of being a "weirdo" to prejudice the appreciation of his music. "That's why I was so pleased that our fans concentrated on our music, which is definitely the main thing in this band," says Boy George.

Culture Club first landed in the U.S. for a quick, two-day get-acquainted look just after the release of their "Kissing To Be Clever" album. Tony Gordon, their manager, had arranged with Epic to throw a bash at Manhattan's Ritz nightclub in December '82. The Ritz was a good showcase, a rock palace for the "in" crowd, musically sophisticated, hip—what in England is called "trendy." Reggae, an important mixture in the Culture Club blend, had a chance to be appreciated there.

The reggae sound had never rolled across the U.S. as it had in England. Outside of New York, Los Angeles and perhaps one or two other cities, reggae was still as unheard of as the birdcall of the hoopoo. One of the things Culture Club managed to achieve in its musical conquest of the American heartland was to penetrate it with this driving Caribbean beat, though with an accent that to purists would seem fulsomely lush and overripe.

This was George's first visit to America. Jon Moss had been to the U.S. before; he had relatives in Los Angeles and had visited there. For Mikey and Roy, as for George, it was new, strange and slightly intimidating.

Boy George found the atmosphere in America more tense than England's. That gave him an insight as to why the Culture Club sound was able to find itself so readily appreciated in the native home of much of the band's music. He said that their music sounded relaxing to American ears, and if by "relaxing" he meant the tuneful and melodic quality they purveyed, he was right.

He was pleased to observe that in New York people for the most part weren't "freaked" on account of his appearance. People had told him, "When you go to New York, people are going to react differently to you." He did get some "ugly stares," but he got those in England, too, so they didn't particularly rattle him.

Two experiences he had in New York stuck in his mind after he returned to England. One was the girl outside the Ritz who offered him a bunch of purple roses—he had never seen purple roses before. The other occurred the day after the performance at the Ritz, when he was walking with some of the "club" members in Central Park. People came up to them, "really ordinary guys," Boy George recalled, and said, "We loved the music." He was thrilled by the tribute. "They didn't mention the way we look."

The first real U.S. tour began two months later. It was a far more complex, lavish and extended affair. The band would play twenty cities from coast to coast. By the tour's end, Boy George had become a household word. Three hits from his first album, which in its U.S. release included "Time," were getting so much play that almost each flick of the radio dial would vault his voice into the American air.

Tony Gordon had orchestrated this tour like a precision march. Just before the band left England, Boy George conducted telephone interviews with three big U.S. dailies, the *Philadelphia Enquirer*, *Detroit Free Press* and *Chicago Tribune*. The press and film crews almost became a part of Culture Club's entourage as the band proceeded from city to city.

The interviews were always conducted from the hotel and scheduled like clockwork. As one interview was being done, the next one would be readied, the reporter slipping into the room the moment it was clear so that Boy George wouldn't waste a minute in between. It was one, two, in and out.

As in England, the American newspaper and TV reporters found Boy George a most ready talker, a journalist's dream, with an opinion on everything and a flow of articulation that seemed inexhaustible:

Has success changed you?

"I think there's this whole myth that when a rock singer becomes successful suddenly he becomes beautiful. But I still wake up with the zits."

What are your favorite books?

"I don't read books generally. The only book I've ever read was the story of Tallulah Bankhead and that was great fun."

Who else would you like to work with?

"I would dearly like to work with Dolly Parton. I would like to do a duo with her. I find that would be more of a challenge for me. But then, you know, I'd like to work with Michael Jackson; but there's got to be a right time."

Are you rich yet?

"Well, I suppose I am, though I haven't seen it yet. I still live in the same place. Again it's all relative. Three years ago I was lucky to make thirty dollars a week, so in that sense I am doing better. But however big you are, you don't see any return in the first year or so. I just don't want to get mean like a lot of people in this business."

Your style really sounds like Motown, and much more.

"With anything of good quality, you take an element of this or that for yourself. You beg, borrow and steal and you use it in a different way. I mean it's like when people compare us to the Beatles. Culture Club is Culture Club, and I've never really gone out of my way to be somebody else. But musically my roots are definitely in R&B, and lots of rock and roll as well."

130

What are your morals?

"I believe that lots of young people have just gone off drugs and sex now. I think people are going back to morals. I don't think they want to hurt each other anymore."

What kind of sex life do you have?

"Really, I'm far too busy for sex at the moment, trying to finish the record. And it's the same on the road—you get up early, travel for hours, stagger into a hotel, rush off to sound-check, do the gig and get back knackered and fall asleep before it all happens again the next day. Anyway, I don't sleep around, and I never did. For a start, I'm not interested in herpes! I'm very moralistic and traditional."

When was the last time you slept with somebody?

"I haven't slept with anyone for two years. I never sleep when I have sex. I usually try to stay awake."

Do you ever remove the Maybelline and comb out your hair?

"I never comb my hair, but I generally wear makeup. There are certain places where I feel I can completely let myself go. But on the whole I don't generally go without makeup. It's a very personal thing with me. I mean, I just hate to look at my face without makeup."

And so it went on that first tour. Boy George made good copy, so the press liked him. But ultimately it was Culture Club and their sound and the *voice* of Boy George that had to establish their credentials. The band's very first gig, at the Malibu on Long Island, showed Boy George that in America things were a little different.

The Malibu, a very small club, was filled with a sold-out crowd, half of which was there to see the band while the other half was there merely to be seen. In England, Culture Club had been used to playing before a mass of screaming kids infected with a fever akin to the Beatlemania of the sixties. Culture Club would never be able to evoke this sort of response during their American concerts. Americans recognized in Culture Club a "new music" band with a '65 sound, a good dance band, with one decided showstopper, Boy George.

At the Malibu, the band was well-received, though at one point the noise from the floor climbed to the level where England's top crooner was compelled to shout a vigorous, "Shut up!" On this tour, Culture Club had been augmented by keyboardist Phil Pickett, saxophonist Steve Grainger and the inimitable Helen Terry. The reviews it received on this first date would be duplicated pretty much by similar favorable reviews in other cities.

About Boy George's vocals: "Popular music hasn't heard a more gifted voice in years."

About Culture Club: "The band was excellent with the addition of a two-man horn section and a female backup vocalist filling out the sound."

Their appearance at New York's Palladium, a far larger house, was equally successful. Blasé New Yorkers complimented Boy George on knowing how to keep an audience's attention. He appeared on stage barefoot and clad in a dress and jacket. He twirled and danced, clutching the dolls and flowers that pelted the stage. A reviewer summed it up: "His insane ballet can only be described as . . . well, Boy George."

After the Palladium show, Epic threw a huge party at Mr. Chow, a swank East Side restaurant. It was the first U.S. press party for Boy George. A mob clustered at the entrance and it was with difficulty breasted by the guests. The Epic execs had to buffet their way through the throng. A giant six-foot-six doorman named George looked down at the other George, in whose honor the party was being held, and asked, "Who are you?" It took a few minutes before the matter got straightened out and Big George permitted Boy George to enter.

Among the guests at Mr. Chow were Carol Baker, Steve Winwood, Jann Wenner of Rolling Stone and Erin Moran, "Joanie" of "Happy Days." Erin said she'd "never seen anyone quite as sexy as Boy George." It was quite a bash, but in the middle of the festivities Boy George got up and, with robes flowing, departed with Jon Moss into a waiting limo.

Boy George surprised everybody by his disinterest in seeing the sights or even meeting famous personalities. One day at Elaine's, an Upper East Side hot spot, Jon Moss was thrilled to discover Woody Allen sitting at one of the tables, but Boy George did not react in the slightest. It was the same at the Russian Tea Room, Boy George's favorite place in New York, where he had the best table, the second booth; Sylvester Stallone was in the first booth, but again Boy George concentrated chiefly on the food.

Food, in fact, especially dessert, was one of Boy George's chief temptations in the U.S. "You eat a lot here," he observed. "I've eaten non-stop since I got here. I'm just turning into a huge blob."

Boy George's first extended exposure to the U.S. had been preceded by certain qualms on his part concerning his safety. On account of his flamboyant appearance he had been alarmed as to the possibility of maniacal violence, which the English press portrays as being rampant on American streets, especially in New York. "When I came to America I thought I was going to get shot," he admitted, though he realized soon enough that his fears had been exaggerated. With relief he noted, "I walked down the street and didn't see one gun. I think people just misinterpret the way things are."

While in New York, Boy George and Jon Moss went on

a clothes-buying spree at Bloomingdale's, shopping in different departments. At the beginning of the tour, Boy George wore mostly the creations of Vivian Westwood, a British designer who does big, shapeless clothes, which, despite their raggedy look, cost as much as $1,500. George's chief guide on his shopping expeditions in New York was Susan Blond, a top publicity exec at Epic, who proved so helpful that he told one New York rock magazine that not he, but Susan Blond, was "going to be *the* Superstar of the '80s."

Susan Blond eased Boy George's introduction to the U.S. She found Boy George one of the most marvelous people she'd ever known in the record business. "I can make people famous whether I like them or not," Susan said, "and have many times." She adored Culture Club personally, and especially Boy George. Making the British pop star famous was an easy task, because he already had "such a definite image. Plus," Susan added, "he is the nicest person."

Susan arranged for photographs by the famous Francesco Scavulo, who had photographed such beauties as Cheryl Tiegs, Christy Brinkley, Carol Alt and Bianca Jagger. She found Boy George the easiest person to work with. "We could do fashion, we could do *Vogue, Interview*, plus the rock papers, any TV, because anything he says is interesting and original."

As the Culture Club caravan rolled across America in less than three hectic weeks, a tight organization was maintained. The musicians traveled in unmarked Econoline vans, which kept in touch by radio, so that Helen Terry and Phil Pickett in one van could communicate with the rest of the band spread over several others. They decided not to travel in limos to avoid being obvious. Sometimes, in places like Toronto, hundreds of kids would be surrounding the dressing rooms. As they moved around the country all the band members had secret names. Boy George's was "Ed Berringer."

In the theatres they usually moved through back elevators and kitchens. Just prior to going on stage he would be fully dressed and made up, applying his lipstick only at the very last moment. Once he went out on the streets without makeup and was surprised that several people recognized him.

There were no incidents throughout the tour. Boy George's fear of the South proved as groundless as his erstwhile fear of New York. Epic received only one threatening letter. At the end, Boy George would sum up, "It was fantastic, and we preferred playing America to anywhere else."

During his first tour Boy George had suffered one disappointment. It had nothing to do with the concerts or the success of his appearances. Much to his embarrassment, being a perfectionist in these matters, Culture Club's first smash album in the U.S. had, in his eyes, a flaw.

"The record company in America decided they would stick "Do You Really Want To Hurt Me?" as the first track on side one," he complained when he returned for his second tour. "They chopped around the running order. Believe me, it was never to be intended like that. It was paced beautifully, and they chopped it up and moved it around."

Coming back to America in the late fall of '83 would be easier than the first tour. First, he felt that Culture Club no longer had to prove itself, and second, he enjoyed the sense of achievement that came from being in the country where rock music, being a native growth, had a more enduring quality than it had in England, where a success one day could be blown away the next.

Yet, even as he spoke these words, much of the traditional concepts of American music had been changed,

135

due to the advent of MTV, Music Television, the rock music cable channel which now determined pretty much what music would last and what would die. Culture Club's first hit in the U.S. was threatened for a brief period with the latter fate due to MTV's displeasure over the video.

MTV uses musical videotapes supplied by record promoters the way a radio stations uses records. Several million viewers during the past year became acquainted with some twenty-five "new music" groups by watching their videos on the MTV cable. Greg Geller, A & R vice president at Epic, says, "MTV has a drastic effect on the way we evaluate artists. It's why an Adam Ant makes such an impact—his look and the look of his videos."

MTV did not at first like the look of the video for "Do You Really Want To Hurt Me?" It did not want to play the Culture Club hit because it thought the video too "soft" for them, that is, not exactly "album oriented radio" (AOR), which is what MTV follows.

Another reason why MTV balked was its objection to ethnic references. On the video were black people portraying minstrels. MTV felt that could be interperted as racist. The cable company further objected to the Hebrew lettering on the band's costumes. Boy George couldn't come up with a clear answer as to what the letters meant. He said the Hebrew writing had been chosen "because it just looks pretty." At last, when the song was already a Top Five single, MTV showed a different version of the video.

Making videos is not Boy George's favorite part of the music business. "It's like traveling to work on a bus—it's a bit of a drag," because they take a long time to produce and Boy George doesn't like to be bored. He wasn't happy with the first couple he worked on. But he really liked the videos for "Miss Me Blind" and "It's A Miracle," for both of which he wrote the scripts.

The video for "Miss Me Blind" is about a Japanese girl who falls for a Western pop star, but it's really about the "platonic friendship" Boy George has recently developed in real life for four-foot-five-inch Miko, a Japanese girl who shares his London home and instructs him in the delicate art of Oriental customs. Miko has inspired him with a Japanese phrase as the title for Culture Club's next album, which in English means, "Wake up with a house on fire." The same idea occurs at the end of the "Miss Me Blind" video, where "the house on fire" is being put out by boys wielding guitars.

The video for "It's A Miracle" also has the Japanese motif, as well as the Japanese girl, this time built around a board game showing "all the achievements we've had," Boy George says.

George recalls one very nice moment in the making of a video: "We did a video called 'Kiss Across The Ocean,' and we filmed the fans for about two hours," he says. "Before the show a lady went out with a camera and asked the girls what would they do with Boy George if they had a half-hour with him, and everyone of them said, 'have a conversation.' Not one of those kids said they wanted to go to bed with me and rip off my clothes. That makes me feel very optimistic."

Though Boy George's second U.S. tour with Culture Club turned out to be a rousing success, which saw him chatting on many of the major TV talk shows and socializing with Hollywood stars, it got off to a bad start. Boarding the plane at London's Heathrow Airport, the usual army of photographers and fans was lying in wait for him. Unlike the old "poser" days, he was now rapidly losing patience with the camera-clicking reporters.

His dress for the $2,000 Concorde flight to Washington,

D.C. consisted of green socks, a black kaftan and just a touch of makeup. He had hurried to make the flight. When he saw the photographers he did something he rarely does—he shouted, shaking his handbag, "There is no way you vultures are going to get my picture today." For this outburst, one paper dubbed him "Blue Boy George." He explained: "How many times can you be photographed in a paper just for catching a plane?" Being photographed all the time, Boy George complained, "is boring, boring, boring."

By the time he arrived in Washington he'd calmed down, and regretted his loss of temper. He said, "Do you know, I was up half the night sewing sequins on my band's costume? I was tired when I arrived at Heathrow. I'd been up at six o'clock."

Culture Club's second U.S. tour was comparatively short—only ten days. This period was fitted into a general touring schedule of European dates that gave an indication of the world-wide popularity of the English pop star. For instance, after flying back to the U.K. from the last American show in Denver's Red Rocks Amphitheatre on September 12, Culture Club was scheduled to appear on Italian TV the very next day, starting a string of dates throughout Europe that would take them right along almost to the end of the year. Afterwards there would be Australia, Japan, Thailand and then, in the spring, back on the American continent, starting in Montreal, Canada.

Despite the smash hits from the new "Colour By Numbers" album to be released a few weeks later, the sound of Culture Club—"black-and-white pop for child-ears," Boy George called it—was decidedly overshadowed by the personality of the singer. America this time around treated him as a "celebrity." His makeup kit again proved of more fascination to the public and the press than the band's music. Again and again he was forced to address it in interview after interview—the topic just would not go away.

The other burning question being put to him repeatedly in different forms was, "What do you think about kids trying to look like you?"

In Atlanta, Boy George gave his most explicit answer to this question:

"Most kids when they go to a fancy dress party go as somebody really obvious, like Cinderella or a pirate. Most people haven't got imagination. Most people are very limited in their imagination. And for most kids it's as much as they can do to dress up like me. It proves out easier, you know.

"I was talking to my manager's daughter a couple of months ago. She asked me for an idea of such a fancy dress, and I said cover yourself in tins and go as a supermarket. But of course she didn't want to do that, because she wanted to look pretty. And most people look at Boy George and the image that Boy George has is someone very pretty. It's almost like a doll. A lot of kids make dolls of me. It's a very, very easy image to have.

"You know, a kid can go into the kitchen and rip off a dishcloth, stick on a hat and become Boy George. And really that's as far as most kids can go in being individual. I don't think clothes make the person. I think really it is the personality, the character. . . .

"I think what we're saying is to make the kids think about different things, to make them think about fascism, to make them think about tough guys, and all these kinds of social rituals that we have to live through. How many people enjoy school? I mean, how many people in the audience have actually enjoyed their time in school? In England we don't encourage kids to enjoy school. In America it's a different kind of system altogether. Kids do enjoy school, more than they do in England."

Culture Club's second U.S. tour played to full houses in ten cities. There were a number of stirring moments that blazoned the name of Boy George into the pages of the newspapers. The first incident occurred in New York, where Boy George publicly denounced the Plaza Hotel, where the band was booked. "The employees of the Plaza thought we were garbage off the street," he complained. "Then someone asked for our autographs and suddenly we got our rooms."

Added Jon Moss, "When we walk into hotels, people always expect the worst. But we don't smash up hotels like some rock stars do. We're very nice boys. I'm very happy to say we've got a great reputation around the world."

A personally embarrassing moment occurred in Philadelphia. As Boy George recalled it afterwards: "I had a costume change and came on with a hanger on the back of my coat. . . . I think the most embarrassing thing was having it in a newspaper photo the next morning. . . . Another time we had a costume change in the middle of 'Church Of The Poison Mind.' I came out of my dressing room, and one of my coats was in one room and the other in the other.

"I was running around with no clothes on screaming at the top of my voice, 'Where's my clothes!' It was really embarrassing. I came on covered in safety pins."

The most publicized event of the tour occurred in connection with Boy George's appearance on the "Tonight Show." Boy George came on wearing a bedspread he got in Barcelona. He talked with Joan Rivers, who was hosting the show, about the bedspread he wore. "People usually grow out of dressing up. I've grown into it. I never go looking ordinary. There are too many people already doing that." The two hit it off surprisingly well, considering the sharp tongues of both parties. "I never have excuses for the way I look," Boy George informed the "Tonight" host. "You don't get Boy George saying, 'OK, I've created a person, and he's the freak and I'm normal.'"

"I am the freak."

16

Boy George
Today

Boy George today is a millionaire. A celebrity. A superstar.

Ten years ago he began "dressing up" because he wanted to be noticed. Today at twenty-two, he has achieved his goal. Not a day goes by in England without his name being mentioned—not just in the media, but in the pubs, on the trains, in the homes, in the places of work and, quite possibly, in the royal palace.

Wonders are attributed to him. A twelve-year-old girl regained consciousness from a coma in which she lay for three weeks after doctors began to play tapes of Boy George.

His slightest whim becomes a reality. When a German sports company asked him to design a running shoe, he drew a model of a pair of platform running shoes on a serviette as a joke. The next day they turned up with them and he wore them on stage.

Boy George is so famous today that he can turn down an invitation for a royal command performance.

Awards are showered on him. An international women's organization voted him one of the world's ten most desirable bachelors. The Milliners' Society of England awarded him "Hat of the Year." He's been voted one of the Ten Worst Dressed Women of the Year. The British Phonograph industry voted him and Culture Club 1983's top performers.

Wherever he goes he creates a sensation. Stopped by French customs for being dressed as a Japanese geisha girl, he said, "No one is going to push Boy George around on such a flimsy pretext."

An American teacher sent him a doll dressed as him and said that she was going to use him as an example to her pupils of how normal people should behave.

In England an anti-George movement is under way. One man wrote a newspaper that Boy George was "driving him stark, raving mad." He kept seeing Boy George's face—even in his sleep.

London's nightclubs are full of foreign photographers looking for the Boy George-inspired fashions.

Boy George's father claims his son is a lot tougher than he appears to be from the clothes and makeup. "If George belted you, you'd know about it," he says.

The object of all this excitement today lives in an unpretentious mews cottage in London's St. John's Wood. He shares his home with an eighteen-year-old roommate and with Miko, the tiny Japanese girl who has taught him how to use chopsticks and inspired him with a love for all things Japanese. According to a friend, "George has gone completely overboard for the Japanese way of life."

According to his roommate, Boy George is very tidy and houseproud. "When he's on the phone he picks all the dirt off the carpet," he says. "And his bedroom is full of soft cuddly toys."

Outside his home, flocks of young girls are always parked on his doorstep. When they find that someone has chalked a message on his wall, they wash it off. Sometimes, to obtain a glimpse of their idol, they embolden themselves to ring his bell and ask if they can use his toilet. Sometimes Boy George will invite a group of them in for tea.

At home Boy George likes to lounge around in a kimono. He spends a lot of time arranging his collection of dolls. His most precious acquisition has been a signed etching of himself by David Hockney. He relaxes by watching his favorite TV program, "Coronation Street."

He keeps busy recording Culture Club's next album. He is working with Roy Hay on writing and recording the soundtrack to "The Electric Dream," a film being shot in San Francisco. It's about a computer that writes songs. There's also talk of Boy George acting in a movie. "In a lot of ways I'm very humorous, too, a bit like Liberace or Charlie Chaplin," he says.

Boy George is also writing songs for others. He's written a song for Tina Turner and one for the group Musical Youth. He and Roy Hay have written all the songs for Helen Terry's album.

One of Boy George's greatest pleasures has been bringing his mother and father on several tours. His mother has been to the Vatican and to Ireland. "She wanted to go and see the Pope," Boy George says. "I couldn't arrange an audience with him."

But despite all his activities, wealth and status, Boy George is said to be unhappy. Recently he told a British newspaper, "I am a recluse already. Years ago I used to love going to clubs and all that. Now I much prefer having a quiet life. If I go out at all I'll go to a small restaurant."

The only place where Boy George today seems to be able to really relax is at his parents' place. His mum says that he loves to come home. "He can walk around without his makeup on and get away from all the pressure."

17

Boy George
on Boy George

"Well, I am emotional. I love to cuddle, hold hands—silly things like that. I suppose at the end of the day I could sit in all the time and watch the colour tv."

On Character and Stardom...

"Character's something you have to create, you can't get it by dressing up. I like old women that you meet at bus stops. They're characters, it's not someone who comes up to you and says I was punk in '76. Remember that old rigmarole?"

On Morals...

"I've got very good morals. That's very important in a rock star because most of them have no principles whatsoever. They're all going 'round insulting chauffeurs and throwing televisions out of hotel windows. I'm not from the old school of rock stars—'You scratch my back, I'll scratch yours.' The most boring thing in music are the clichés, and mixing with other rock stars is generally boring. It's a real cliché, like Beverly Hills and credit cards and all that. I don't like rock stars. I belong where I am. I enjoy doing what I'm doing and it works.

"It works very well, in fact. 'Kissing To Be Clever' placed three singles in the Top Ten—an amazing feat for a debut—and 'Colour By Numbers' looks set to do just as well."

On His Appearance...

"Obviously I'm into myself, but I'm not walking around just saying, Oh everybody look at me, look at me. I wear makeup and dress this way because it makes me look better. I'm not doing it to get people to stare at me. If I wanted to do that I could just put a pot on my head, wear a wedding dress and scream down the High Street. It's easy just to get attention.

"That's what people think they're doing. People also think that if you look like this you're running away from

148

something, and that's a load of rubbish as well. I'm not hiding. It's a long way from hiding. I really don't think that there's anything wrong with wanting to make yourself look as good as possible. I'm not just a person who wears makeup. There is a lot more that goes into it.

"I tell you, I really hate decadence. I hate people who really think they're risqué and daring."

On Aggression...

"Of course, I get annoyed. I'm a human being, I'm not a star."

On Success...

"I'm not frightened of not being successful, I'm frightened of not being successful as a person. I'd much rather that people think, 'Oh, he's a happy person,' rather than, 'Wow, isn't he clever?' Because I'm not. It's all luck and what you make of it.

"The only nice thing is that if a housewife comes up to you in the street and says I like your record, you feel much better than if someone with a really sickly sneer on his face says, 'Ooh, congratulations, it's sooo good.' You just really want to punch him.

"I know why people hate me. The thing is, if you go to the Palace, those people are very normal. I'm not saying they're idiots because they dress up or they don't dress up, but their reasons for doing it are very silly.

"I don't want to be a boring pop star, I don't want to be a rock star, and I never will be. How could I? I take this seriously enough to want to be a success, but if it fails I'm not going to fold away and not be able to go out. I'm not going to hide. I'm just not desperate."

On Love . . .

"I'm not here as a sexual crusader. I'm not encouraging people to be like me. I'm saying 'Go out and find love, what's true to you.' Love is more important than anything."

"I am what I am."

"I don't think you ever know yourself. That's why I think most psychiatrists or analysts are a waste of time. All I know is I'm not like [David Bowie's] Ziggy Stardust. I haven't created a stage persona. I am what you see."

On Dressing Up . . .

"Dressing ordinary is boring. I did modeling for two years so I have a feel for makeup and clothes.

"I'm interested in being a personality and to get people's attention you have to be more than a musician. You need something that captures you on TV.

"At first they seemed quite wary of releasing us in the States. They didn't want my pictures on the album jacket.

"In Britain, you can become a minor celebrity without actually doing anything, if you just have a weird haircut or clothes. So I started by going out of my way to be as outrageous as possible. I had no money, but I would go everywhere for free, just chatting my way in."

"In Japanese Kabuki theatre it's considered to be of great cultural significance and beauty for a man to appear as a woman.

"I'm a big guy. If I tried to be a woman it would be disgusting. What people don't understand is that I'm not satisfying some desire to be a woman by dressing the way I do. I'm doing it because I enjoy it."

On Copycats...

"What always happens with an eccentric fashion is it gets watered down and made normal. You'll probably see it in Bloomingdale's someday.

"I think the sad thing is people can't bear to credit me with it. We went to a store in London just before we left and I took a skirt off the rack which was a complete copy of one of the designs we had in my shop before we started Culture Club.

"Every time I open the *Daily Mail* there's some debutante

151

with dreadlocks and ribbons in her hair. I want to know why they're not saying it's derivative from what we're doing. I mean I'm honest about our music. So give us some fashion credits."

The Norm, Fear and Fashion

"I'm just a normal person. I'm not an Andy Warhol, I'm not a concept. I'm just a normal Hello John from down the road.

"I've got beliefs, but I don't mean that's it, black and white, and that's all you should believe from me. Confidence comes and goes, it's a human thing."

On U.S. Success . . .

"I think any successful band is a mixture of things. Obviously, it's got a lot to do with music. It's also got a lot to do with the way we look—more the way I look. I think people have become very interested in that. They're quite intrigued with it and they want to know more about it.

"Either people dismiss you or they become involved in what you're doing. And I think people have become involved. Obviously, we're not as successful as we'd like to be because this is just the first album. This means nothing in a way. There's kind of a long way to go. It's okay having one hit album and maybe three hit singles, but I'd quite like to have a few more. So there's still a large amount of hard work to do."

On Grammy's...

"When I made my comment on the Grammy Awards the next day they had colleges doing debates on it. It upset people.

"I do these things deliberately, because last year I think I was in danger of becoming the next Queen Mother. I had to put a stop to that. That's why I rock the boat from time to time...."

On God...

"I've got a Catholic background but I'm not religious. I don't believe in God, God as a person that is, but I believe in the spirit. I don't believe that there's somebody up there with a bowl of rice waiting to feed us. I believe in life after death. I think that we all go back into the earth, really, I don't think that we actually come back as another person but we all end up as maggots and that sort of thing. After all, we fertilize the earth, don't we? We must come from something. It's a bit naive to think that we don't live again in some form.

"How can you just go away? Nobody's proved how man started, so nobody can prove how man ends. But then I don't wish to die, it's the last thing in my mind."

On School . . .

"I hated school. I was called a snob at school because I talked 'proper.' I was good at art, English and poetry, but my best subject was religious education. I was outrageous, I suppose. I dyed my hair and wore makeup, but only eyeliner!

"They weren't supposed to let you annoy them, but I used to sit there saying 'You're ugly, I hate your guts.'

"I was ridiculed by both boys and masters. But it gave me the strength to confront society."

On Image . . .

"I'm constantly being asked if my image fits in with the traditional forms of music we play—will we sell to hamburger queens and truckers' sons all over the West. Yet the way I look at it is very obviously contradictory to that. I think this is very good. I like contradictions. There's a line from 'Do You Really Want To Hurt Me?' that says, 'Everything's not what you see,' which is basically what I believe. It's kind of boring when things are just what they are, don't you think?

"The differences don't exist to me, because they nick each other's ideas so much. There's so much similarity between classic rock songs and classic R&B songs that it's pathetic to say a white man can't do soul or a black man can't do rock. The barriers are breaking down slowly, and

154

I'm proud that Culture Club has contributed to that, because that's what we're about."

What Turns Boy George On...

"Their breath. If people have got horrible breath I can't stand them. If someone's got a nice smelling mouth I always tell them. That's what turns me on. And hands, nice warm hands that make you feel all childish."

How Boy George Got His Hat...

"Jon bought it for me."

On Culture Club's Music...

"It could be taken as pretentious but it's a very basic sound. They're good, structured songs. You don't expect it, but that's what you get."

"You can start a band to write good songs if you can start a band to dress up and have your picture taken. The whole point is that I like the idea of things not being what they seem."

On Songwriting . . .

"I never write about boys and girls, or men and men, or whatever. I hate those, 'My baby left me, wah, wah, diddy diddy dum dum' songs."

On "Colour By Numbers" . . .

"It's very vocal. People might say it's softer than 'Kissing To Be Clever,' but actually it's bigger. There's a lot of harmony, a lot more voice work and a lot of sax this time. It's more acoustic than the last one, not as much electronics. It's a more edible version of 'Kissing.' I'm very pleased with it."

On Being a Celebrity . . .

"I don't feel like a superstar. I had a more glamourous time living on my wits, staying in bed until four and then going to a night club.

"I used to go out in a straw hat covered in birds and fruit. I would not go out without it, because I didn't want to look like other people.

"I did not have a job, but lived as a minor celebrity without any responsibility. Now I have to do everything.

The trouble with being a star is that you don't have time for relationships and they are also too difficult.

"You go on stage to all that adulation and it is very difficult for somebody else in your life to cope with all that.

"I like being on my own but I like meeting fans and talking to them. I feel disappointed to find them still in awe when I meet them a second time."

On Rock...

"I like everything, really! I love Kissing The Pink and New Edition—they're both brilliant. And I also love a lot of the old favorites, like Gladys Knight, Stevie Wonder, T. Rex, Smokey Robinson—they all influenced me."

On Other Stars...

MARC BOLAN:
"He came from the streets. He's my kind of hero."

DOLLY PARTON:
"She's got a lot of affection."

THE POLICE:
"They're very good and they're very very white."

ANNIE LENNOX:

"One of the most exciting things about music is the women. Annie Lennox, I think, is very exciting. To have her number one in America is very exciting. To me, she's got real good spirit. I like that kind of woman. I think it would be quite nice to have a women explosion."

JOHN DENVER:

"I didn't really think I'd like him but he's a nice person. Not just a nice musician—a nice person. I met him in Germany."

JOAN RIVERS, WHO HOSTED "THE TONIGHT SHOW" WHEN HE WAS A GUEST:

"She's my favorite." He even has some potential joke lines she could have used: "I love that dress. I never get tired of seeing it." And "You've got so many lines, you could open a railway station."

JON MOSS:

"As you can see, we're completely different people, one complements the other."

PEARL BAILEY:

"One of my favorite singers. Where most jazz singers project this aura of pain and glory, she is cynical and funny. I like that. The pop world is very fickle. It's really important to remember what you've been and to realize that what you've achieved is not really all."

DIVINE:

"Divine is ugly and disgusting. He's like a kid on the school playground trying to shock people by being as disgusting as possible. I'd rather watch 'Dynasty.'"

Glittering lives of famous people!
Bestsellers from Berkley

★ ★